REJECTION
HURTS

STEVE HEPDEN

CONTENTS

DEDICATION

To Maki, Joy and Frida
who have been loved unconditionally

ACKNOWLEDGEMENTS

Without my wife Chris this book would not have been written. To help someone who writes as he speaks is one thing but to help someone who writes as he preaches is something else. The words still ring in my ears, "you've said this before" or "what do you mean?" It has been for me a fairly long challenging time but think of Chris putting up with me for a couple of years presenting her with chapter after chapter and change after change and query after query. She had been brilliant.

Thank you...

To Deanna Francis for her faithfulness throughout the writing of the book in giving such good advice and clarity on the intricacies of syntax and grammar.

To Myra Lockhart for her help by casting her discerning eye over the manuscript.

To my good friend David Powell who took on the task of publishing the book. I am indebted for his advice, management and direction.

To my dear Rhino friends who in their own inimitable way, have brought much encouragement to me with their love and care, which inspired me to complete the book.

To the many friends and acquaintances that have given support and encouragement.

Endorsements

Rejection is such a huge heart issue, crippling multitudes of people and no doubt affecting us all. In this book 'Rejection Hurts', Steve Hepden will help you diagnose your issues, and then map out a way for you to come into acceptance, forgiveness and love. So helpful; so freeing; so life giving.

John Arnott
Catch the Fire Toronto & Partners In Harvest International

We all know rejection hurts but its painfulness makes it hard to understand and even worse to deal with. This book is wise but not complicated, down to earth and rooted in personal experience. Steve has created an understandable and practical guidebook to the past, an explanation of the present situation and a route map into a better future. He knows that to accomplish this, we need the best kind of companion - the friendship of a God who loves us. I commend it.

Eric Delve
Evangelist and Teacher, UK

This is a wonderful combination of pastoral and practical insights into the power and effects of rejection in today's society. Through story telling and compelling biblical insights Steve offers a wealth of resources to transform the negative equity of rejection into opportunities to find healing and wholeness.

Rev Dr Russ Parker
2Restore: Healing Wounded Churches, Farnham, UK

With a lovely mix of compassion, skill, and scriptural insight, Steve takes us into the complex world of rejection, and gently shows us the way to the remarkable healing grace that is available in Christ. I feel so blessed to be Steve's friend, and have often benefited from his ministry, through which many of my own wounds of rejection have found healing.

Rev Canon Michael Mitton
St Paul's, Derby, UK

A comprehensive and thorough look at the business of rejection and how we overcome the hurt and pain of it. Sensitive, compassionate and extremely helpful. I commend this book to you.

Nick Battle
Gravel Road Trust, Cornwall, UK

PREFACE

It was in 1992 that 'Explaining Rejection' was published. Since then the problem with rejection has not disappeared. In today's climate of such difficulties in family life, together with economic, social and religious problems the world faces including the conflicts affecting so many nations, rejection has undoubtedly affected many more people.

With this in mind, plus the fact that over the years I have experienced and learnt so much more, it seems it is the time to revise and update the previous book. I have used the basis of 'Explaining Rejection' to do this and what has been produced is a much larger book, which includes some previous material.

Please consider too that the book is written from my perspective, experience and sometimes my own terminology. Any names I have used have been changed for the sake of anonymity and confidentially.

This is a book, not only written for those who are living with rejection and need help, but is also for those in a more recovered position who need encouraging to move on. In addition, I hope can be a help to those who are involved in counselling and prayer ministry.

As you read this updated version of 'Explaining Rejection', remember that I am looking for understanding and hopefully some revelation to you personally.

I trust you will be enlightened and challenged.

Steve Hepden
February 2016

INTRODUCTION

Just up the road from our church was a large house that used to be an orphanage. Many of the children who had lived there would most probably have been suffering from some form of rejection. They needed love, affection and approval but had been deprived of this. Although the staff did what they could to provide a secure environment for these poor children, what they could not give was the loving, nurturing care within a family unit that every child needs.

Into this world of rejection came a little three-year-old girl called Grace. She was literally left at a railway station because she was not wanted by either of her parents. In fact they fought over her, not because they wanted her but because they did not want her. She was pushed backwards and forwards to each parent until they decided to abandon her. Grace became an orphan with her parents still very much alive. She was taken into Muller's Homes in Bristol. Some say a child that age would be too young to understand. Maybe intellectually, but the rejection and abandonment she would feel would have affected Grace deeply. She may not have understood but the consequences of that experience were evident in many ways as she grew up.

Sometime later my wife Chris and I were involved in a wedding and were fortunate enough to use the beautiful garden of the former orphanage as part of the reception. Grace, now a young woman, showed me a fire escape at the rear of the garden where her boyfriends used to creep in at night, sleep with her and then get out quickly before matron started her early morning visits. She was desperate for love but faced more rejection than acceptance in her life. She compensated by getting involved in many difficult and very wrong situations that, to her sorrow, only heightened her feelings of rejection and abandonment rather than acceptance and the sense of feeling safe.

There was a boy called Sam of a similar age to this little girl. Sam had six sisters, five who had different fathers with a mix of cultural backgrounds. He was not sure who his father was, which affected his own self-image and self-esteem. There was no sense of love, affection or acceptance and he was left in his rejection, emotionally destitute and impoverished. He grew up very sensitive to life and found it difficult to handle the circumstances that life brought. As a result of this he could not handle relationships so he superficially drifted through various associations, which brought such emotional pain that he decided being alone and isolated was best. When we met him, we soon saw his kindness and compassion but we also saw his inscrutability, for he had become expert at protecting himself against the inevitable pain caused by openness and vulnerability.

Years later Grace and Sam met, fell in love and ultimately married. Chris and I were privileged to help officiate at their wedding and can testify how amazing God has been in restoring and healing broken lives.

Rejection can affect anyone from the womb right through to old age. Most people have felt the sting of rejection in one way or another and as we shall see, there are many causes.

A need for acceptance and belonging is part of the basic instinct of humanity.

Everyone has a deep desire to be accepted. We want people to believe in us and love us unconditionally. Rejection will attempt to undermine this through isolation and abandonment. People also have a longing to belong and this can be seen in the various people groups across the nations, whether tribal or something more Western as in the multitude of clubs that many people belong to such as the diverse areas of sport, etc. There are, in many inner city areas, gangs of young men and women. One of the reasons for this is that many of them have never known their fathers and so try to seek relationship and acceptance in other ways. You do not have to go very far to see the results of rejection. They are all around us.

The events of life continuously highlight the conflict between acceptance and rejection. It is impossible to go through life with everyone being nice to you all of the time. It is how we learn to handle this so that the insidious and menacing power of rejection does not overwhelm. Some say our bodies respond to rejection like they do to physical pain. It is important to remember that you cannot bury your problems dead for when circumstances trigger them, the deep, hidden memories will surface provoked by rejection.

The following illustrations will give some idea of the breadth and depth of this insidious problem.

1. Many years ago, when living in Bristol, Chris and I had a phone call from a woman we did not know. When she arrived at our house it was not difficult to sense the enormity of the problem. She had an overwhelming hatred for her mother. From birth she was not wanted and now she was fifty and in crisis. The hatred was affecting everything in her life. Chris and I knew it was rejection that triggered this. We talked and advised her to not just understand forgiveness but take responsibility and declare forgiveness. This is not easy but Jesus said do not forgive seven times but seventy times seven. (Matthew 18:21-22) In other words, keep on forgiving until the pressure subsides and peace begins to percolate into the rejection. We showed her forgiveness has

to be a lifestyle. She took responsibility and made a choice to forgive. We prayed with her regarding her rejection and ministered healing to the wound within. She then left us knowing there was a way through this longstanding problem.

2.   Once I was involved in praying for a person who was born as a replacement child because of the death of a sibling. He was born to fill the painful gap, but living up to the memory of a dead child is virtually impossible. What has to be considered is that the new child may be compromised in his development resulting in an inability to form an identity separate to that of the dead child. Sometimes whether consciously or unconsciously, the parents can transfer the qualities and characteristics of the dead sibling to the living one. They may want a child of the same sex as soon as possible and even give the subsequent child a name resembling that of the dead child. This can lead to the replacement child not being or feeling loved for who he is in his own unique identity and personality. This will also open the way to self-rejection because the child will not feel accepted for who he is. He will be angry with himself and his parents. He will feel unwanted and that he was only born as a substitute for a dead brother or sister. He will feel rejected for who he is and hate himself.

3.   The two world wars have produced much emotional and mental turmoil regarding children born just before hostilities. The father went off to war sometimes for years and when he returned home found a child a number of years older. The child had the love and care of his mother but nothing from the father because he was not there. The father did not know his child and the child wondered why this strange man suddenly appeared in the home and stayed! The void created by the 'missing' father's love opened a door for rejection and made things very difficult when the he returned. The problem is the lack of nurture from the father in those early impressionable years

It is a fact that many men returned physically well but unwell in their emotions and mind because of what they saw and experienced of the horrors of war. Often they found it difficult to express love and the child would sense rejection from the father. That could take root affecting him in the years to come. "My father did not love me." "He did not show me his love." "He does not like me." The father probably has no idea of the turmoil going on in the child's mind but the issue is real and the child will suffer rejection.

4. Domination, particularly by a father will ultimately wound a child and give a perspective of "I have to obey him to please him otherwise he will reject me." This will also lead to fear of rejection or even rebellion, resentment and anger. There is no doubt my father loved me, but he could not or did not show it. There is no doubt I loved my father, but it was difficult for me to show my feelings. He insisted that I vote a certain way, read a certain newspaper or take a job that he was satisfied with. He was reactive when Chris' dad helped us with our first car, which was an old Ford bought for the princely sum of £35! If I obeyed him things would be ok but if not, disapproval was clearly shown. Chris reminded me that when we visited my parents I would talk to my father whilst reading the newspaper. It was as though I was putting up a barrier to self-protect. I have learned that this was a fear of rejection stimulated by the thought of being dominated again. Today I am free from the influences of that type of rejection and can write freely about my father. God is good.

5. When Chris and I were working in a Ministry Centre in the UK one of the young people we met was waiting for her exam results. She achieved nine A and one B grade passes. Her father said, "What about the B?" No congratulations, no pleasure and no parental pride, just a sense of rejection that came from a perfectionist father. He was very good at moving the goalposts or changing the rules. It was always a bit more, always pressure to do better, and the fear of failure coupled with the fear of rejection kept his daughter under severe pressure. When she did do well, he did not give her credit in any way. We prayed and continued to counsel her and she began to see a way out.

6.   A figure of speech in which a spoken phrase can be understood in either of two ways is known as a 'double entendre.' One of the interpretations is rather obvious whereas the other is clever but quite often vulgar and sexually suggestive. The Oxford English Dictionary describes a double entendre as being used to 'convey an indelicate meaning.' When I was in the sixth form in school I made an innocent statement in the Geography A level class. The handful of students, mostly my friends, and teacher broke out in loud laughter. I had no idea what I had said until the sudden realisation came and I felt embarrassment, failure and rejection. It was desperately humiliating and for a while I struggled with self-rejection as I tried to get over it. It must have been a powerful moment because I can recall every detail today, particularly the laughter. Happily, it does not affect me now those fifty plus years later and I can remember in peace because the rejection has gone and I can connect to the peace of Christ.

7.   I think the earliest age I have heard of a child being sent to boarding school was around four. I was listening to Radio Bristol and heard the incredulous reactions. Over the years we have prayed with mostly men who were sent to boarding school when they were under ten years old, an age when they needed their parents love and acceptance and not to be sent away feeling forsaken, abandoned and rejected.

8.   If you have been told you were not wanted time and time again, there will come a time when you will react to the feelings of rejection. The tongue has the power of death as well as the power of life (Proverbs 18:21). As a child, if we are trained in a negative way, as we get older it becomes more difficult to turn away from it (Proverbs 22:6). This nagging pressure of rejection will ultimately undermine identity and create a deep emotional wound in our lives. Over the years we have prayed with many people who carry this rejection, which easily connects to fear of further rejection, failure and self-protection, creating a barrier to protect from further negative talk. Continual negative words can become a curse when consistently spoken. A curse is basically 'a wish of evil or misfortune' against a person and although we live in the 20th century, it is very much with us. This will need to be broken in the name of Jesus.

9.   Chris and I have met and ministered to both men and women who were told they were not wanted because their parents wanted the opposite sex from them. To be told you are the wrong sex is devastating; however, for parents to hide this and treat the child as the opposite sex is beyond deception. The pain of rejection and self-rejection results in self-hatred and anger at parents and can be severe. "They do not want me, they wanted a boy/girl." Carrying this into adolescence can bring gender issues that will undermine our God given identity.

10. Were you ever told either in school or by your family members that you were no good and stupid and that you would never make anything in life? As these words become more personalised children have been known to behave in a no good and stupid way as they feel rejection. Teachers and parents should bring honest, loving encouragement to children and not continually demoralise them and crush their spirits.

Albert Einstein almost passed for a mentally retarded child because he did not utter a single word until he was four years old. He was unable to read any letters until he was seven years of age. His teachers had already concluded that he was intellectually challenged and even questioned why his parents were sending him to school. However, Einstein grew up to win a Nobel Prize as a great scientist and to change the face of modern physics, as we know it today.

Rejection will attempt to kill off the potential in a young life through negative words but words of life will bring release.

11. The death of someone very close can bring a great sense of loss. The death of a husband or wife, mother or father or child, can sometimes in personal grief bring a feeling of being abandoned. "Why did you have to die?" "I feel you have rejected me, you have abandoned me!" "How will I manage, how will I cope?" "You have let me down." Instead of being able to grieve in a right and Godly way, the whole experience is internalised in a negative manner.

The strength of the grief and rejection brings some people to a point where they feel unable to let the person go. In a strange way they still feel attached to them even though they are gone. It is not difficult at that point to withdraw, look inwards and feel depressed, not wanting to see or communicate with anyone.

12. Although outdated in our culture, illegitimacy can bring a child a sense of rejection in feeling they were not wanted, they were a mistake and maybe should have been aborted. Scripture talks about a curse of ten generations (Deuteronomy 23:2) but if a child receives love and acceptance starting in the womb, this can be averted. Many children did not know they were 'illegitimate' yet rejection was prevalent, which would hinder them in future years.

I was one of those children where my 'illegitimacy' was deliberately hidden from me and it was only revealed to me in a family crisis when I was in my mid-thirties and involved in leading a large church.

As well as rejection, which includes a sense of insecurity, self-protection, defensiveness and anger there is a feeling of being an 'orphan.' Biblically 'orphan' means fatherless and coming into the revelation of our Heavenly Father's love and a deeper relationship with him has brought me a delightful freedom!

13. Why is it that so many men, including male leaders, have a problem with strong women? Strong women are not Jezebels. It is time for this deception to be dealt with once and for all. So many gifted and anointed women have been rejected regarding leadership and various areas of ministry and have remained locked up because of some quirk of interpretation of scripture by insecure male leaders. So many key women struggle with rejection, which makes them question their faith, calling and ministry and basically end up doing nothing, feeling like they are nothing. It is the church that loses out in this area and we see anointed and gifted women who have a calling to leadership blocked, and undermined in their desire to be what God wants them to be.

Women in this context carry pain of rejection, which has been known to leak or overflow in certain situations of deep frustration. Sometimes this can be ammunition to those who will use it for further accusation and confirmation of their interpretation of scripture, but all that happens is a continuation of negativity and a wounding in their spirits. It is almost as though something dies deep inside. This type of rejection is worldwide and the success of the enemy in using good and well-meaning men brings sadness to my heart.

Yet God is doing something miraculous and freeing many women from this area of rejection. With all of the above areas there is hope. This is not some sort of empty wish, but more an eager anticipation that God can and will heal and set free.

The Message translation sums it up well: *'Then Jesus arrived from Nazareth, anointed by God with the Holy Spirit, ready for action. He went through the country helping people and healing everyone who was beaten down by the Devil. He was able to do all this because God was with Him'* (Acts 10:38 MESSAGE).

MEMORY POINTS

- Rejection can affect anyone.
- Rejection can affect you before birth as well as after.
- Rejection will affect our basic human desires such as the need for acceptance and belonging.
- Rejection comes in many forms, situations and circumstances in life to bring destruction.
- The battleground is immense and rejection will attempt to affect key areas in our lives if given a foothold (Ephesians 4:27 NIV).
- We have hope that is eager anticipation, for healing from a loving heavenly Father and our Saviour and Deliverer Jesus.

Abandoned & Alone

'What a man desires is unfailing love' Proverbs 19:22 NIV

Our loving heavenly Father is dependable, reliable, trustworthy, constant and consistent in His unconditional love to us. This love is more unshakeable, limitless and enduring than anyone on this earth can give.

Someone once said that 'God is in search of humanity for love and relationship; God is in pursuit of us!'

God is passionate about coming down to where we are. This is heaven to earth with God amongst us. We talk about going to heaven yet God talks about heaven coming to earth. Building on this will give us such confidence and security about life, as our relationship with God will be one of total acceptance.

DEFINITION

It is important to define, understand and recognise rejection. The original meaning of rejection is to throw away or to throw back.

I have met people who feel as if they have been thrown away. Rejection will make you feel that nobody cares, that you are on your own and have no one. Rejection is powerful enough to make you believe things that actually have not happened in the way you think they have. This is the subtleness of rejection and is something we need to recognise.

Rejection is:
- Refusal - not accepted, approved of, supported or shown love.
- Dismissal - not considered, removal, being sent away.
- Spurning - being ignored.
- Discarded - thrown away.
- Pushed away or aside - this is more hostile and aggressive.
- Shut out - not let in, turned away.
- Forsaken - being abandoned.
- Not accepted - a feeling that someone does not love you or want you.
- Excluded - the act of forcing someone out.
- Driven away - a premeditated act of getting rid of someone.
- Eliminated - purposely cut off.

The above can be literal acts, mind games or emotional pressure. Consider how many of these definitions affect you.

The consequences of rejection are that people ultimately feel or are made to feel imperfect, worthless, unsatisfactory and useless. They feel abandoned, isolated, alone and angry even in a group of friends, because of the loneliness and hopelessness deep inside. It is here that depression will drift in like a dark cloud.

Rejection is a negative and destructive feeling, which distorts and damages our way of life, undermining our perception of who we are. Some people are able to hide it well and keep going in the best way they can, pretending everything is ok. That is called denial. Rejection is a formidable foe!

We all need both stable relationships and acceptable and satisfying interaction in those relationships. If any of those two ingredients are missing rejection will begin to have an effect.

If rejection manifests as an inability to give or receive love or a denial of love, particularly by someone who is considered close such as a parent or sibling, a good friend, or even a pastor or leader, then basic fundamental human motivation begins to be undermined.

Everyone has a strong motivational drive to form and maintain caring relationships but if this is challenged, rejection is reinforced as self-esteem deteriorates. Sometimes the person perceived to give rejection is a parent. The desire for affection, love and care from that parent is undoubtedly powerful, yet it can be broken down by a denial of the factors that build up and bring security in that relationship. This will be devastating to that child and will undoubtedly deeply influence and affect them as they grow into adulthood, for they will carry the wounds of rejection with them.

Rejection can be active, for example by bullying, teasing or ridiculing. It can also be passive, 'the silent treatment,' which is emotional coldness. Some people have an ability to use both and use them well!

The experience of being rejected is subjective and perceived. You know and feel what is happening. The danger is being oversensitive and that can become a problem in itself.

Rejection results from a denial of love. When you are loved you are approved and accepted but when you feel disapproved of, you will be exposed to rejection.

Young children will not understand, but will feel something that will influence their behaviour, the way they think and show emotions. He or she may behave badly to gain attention and acceptance. We have been created to need love. Love will develop personal growth, giving a good sense of esteem and security.

It is important to understand that rejection does not mean there is no love in the home. Often there is some kind of love, but if there's no expression of it in affection, gentle and positive touch or the spoken word that affirms and builds up, rejection will fill that void.

The hurt personality will begin to exhibit behavioural patterns and attitudes such as withdrawing or reacting in anger. If there were a crisis of identity, he would want to protect himself by not letting people too close for fear of further rejection, and may build emotional walls and barriers to give a sense of security.

Attempting to push the problem away does not work. What happens is that the problem is pushed into the subconscious part of the mind. This is denial. You cannot bury your problems dead. They are and always will be, until dealt with, very much alive. Even years of denial make no difference. The pain and wounds will remain until they are faced and healed through the Father's love.

Feeling unloved and unwanted, worthless, valueless, inadequate, inferior and insecure, you stumble through life. Your attitude becomes, "I can not" or "everyone else can but not me" or "I am useless, I do not feel secure in who I am, I have no identity, no role." Guilt and accusation will bombard you and a stronger sense of self-rejection will influence you as the negative words continue. "I have never really liked myself," "If only I was more like him or her." It will become a spiral of negativity.

Three questions come out of this:
- How can a person who feels rejected handle or even receive love, affirmation or affection?
- How can a person who feels rejected sincerely give love to others?

- How can a person who feels rejected accept the unconditional love of God or give love to God?

Sometimes people cannot give love because they have not received love or even understood what love is. How can you receive what you do not recognise? How can you give what you do not possess?

Rejection can affect all relationships and every area of a person's life, wounding deeply the personality and affecting a person's core, the spirit.

Rejection can happen at any time, although the roots often start in childhood or even the womb. It may not be recognised in those early years but rejection is like a seed planted.

MEPHIBOSHETH

It is a miracle that this man survived beyond his early years. He did, but was left with such pain; physically, emotionally and mentally.

As a five year old he was suddenly hit by personal and traumatic events that shaped his life. His father Jonathan, and grandfather, the King (Saul), were killed in battle on the same day.

Mephibosheth was with his nurse and because she was so afraid that the enemy would come to destroy the rest of the family she picked him up and ran to hide him. As she was running something happened that would send a shudder through any family - she dropped him! We have no idea how, but Mephibosheth was so hurt he became crippled in both feet for the rest of his life (2 Samuel 4:4 NIV). He was unable to walk.

A name in the Old Testament context is often full of meaning and would give insight into personalities. Mephibosheth means shame, greatly shamed or son of shame. How amazing, why call yourself shame?' However, he was not called Mephibosheth when he was born. He had a royal name, Merib-Baal (1 Chronicles 9:40) meaning opponent or contender of Baal, the false God. He changed his name! So you have a child named prophetically who was going to oppose idolatry and false gods who is now known as shame! Was the problem so great that it meant a change of name? It seems so. That is not all for he lived in a place called Lo Debar (2 Samuel 9:4). He was in exile, hidden away in this place that means 'the land of nothing, no pasture, no word or no communication.' It was basically a place of no hope, hidden and too far away to be noticed. In his own eyes though, Mephibosheth was in the right place.

What an amazing start to life! Not only crippled but having to hide from an enemy. Surely Mephibosheth was not only hurt physically but mentally and emotionally as well. Look at where he lived for many years. This is the ultimate rejection defined as self-rejection, he hated himself; self-protection, he was hidden away and not prepared to let anyone in anymore; rebellion, he was full of anger and pain.

I know many Mephibosheths today. Many have been crippled but not physically, more emotionally and mentally. Their spirits have been crushed and wounded, controlled by fear. They feel they had no worth or self-esteem and the hurt child, hidden deep inside was lost and afraid.

This is deep shock and trauma.

He was only five years old!

- He was innocent.
- He was not able to understand.
- It was not his fault.
- He was forgotten.
- There was nothing in the present and nothing to look forward to.
- He was severely mentally and emotionally wounded.

- It was alienation and enmity.
- It was as though he was dead.

The suffering was not deserved. It was someone else's responsibility but it left a deep wound within him, to the extent that every day he was afflicted by his condition.

Mephibosheth lost his father, his grandfather, his health and his home all at the same time and it seems that his mother was not there either. Only the nurse is mentioned and who knows how long she stayed with him.

Mephibosheth Lost His Identity

Identity is how we understand ourselves. It is to do with self-image, self-esteem and individuality. It is the answer to the question, "who am I?" It would seem Mephibosheth did not have a low opinion of himself, he had no opinion of himself! He knew he had nothing and was nothing. He lost any understanding of personal value and worth, acceptance and belonging.

He Lost His Family

Mephibosheth was abandoned and alone. He felt rejected and had no hope because he was by himself. There was no family. But where was his mother? Nobody knows. The scripture does not mention her. It is as though she had never been with her son. He had no one and what happened to the nurse? Was there anyone with him?

He Lost His Inheritance

Everything that was rightfully his was taken away. He had nothing and therefore had nothing to look forward to, and certainly no ability to claim his rights, his inheritance. He was hidden and in exile, far away from anyone with no contact or communication.

Mephibosheth was crippled in both feet. Feet symbolise taking possession of that which is yours; claiming the ground, your rightful inheritance. God said to the Children of Israel, *"every place where you set your foot will be yours"* (Deuteronomy 11:24 NIV).

He Was So Angry

Mephibosheth was in so much pain that the anger at various times must have exploded out of him. Probably at other times it was more passive, smouldering away, building up resentment.

Anger is a major factor in rejection. Even when the person seems afraid or depressed, anger is underneath. It is a root issue we must not neglect, because of its consequences. It seems to be one of the hardest emotions to handle.

Anger is an intense, explosive and destructive emotion. It can be both passive and aggressive. Passive, keeping silent, internalising the anger or aggressive, which can be intimidatory or even violent.

Someone has said, "The more anger towards the past you carry in your heart, the less capable you are of loving in the present."

It all comes back to "what has happened to me?" "I am angry now because of what happened to me thirty years ago." Maybe it is time to deal with the roots. One of the roots of rejection is rebellion, of which anger is a big part and this will lead to intimidation and control. We need to control anger before it controls us.

Yet anger is a necessary human passion. The scriptures clearly say, *'go ahead and be angry. You do well to be angry—but do not use your anger as fuel for revenge. And do not stay angry. Do not go to bed angry. Do not give the Devil that kind of foothold in your life'* (Ephesians 4:26-27 MESSAGE).

Anger is a necessary part of life and common to every person. It is not to be denied, but recognised, understood, accepted and controlled righteously.

It would seem that in his rejection Mephibosheth was angry at everything life had thrown at him, including himself and also King David who he thought wanted to kill him. Later we will see it was not true, for all that David wanted to do in his compassion, love and care, was give him a home and bring restoration.

Some of the greatest needs a person can have are:

- To be loved and know personal worth.
- To be accepted unconditionally without violation of personal conviction.
- To be needed to the point of emotional well being.

Anger will prevail when these needs are not met. Mephibosheth had none of these and was very angry in his rejection.

He Was Extremely Negative In His Thinking And Talking

What would you do if you were in Mephibosheth's state of mind? The thing is you may not be like him, 'as bad as him' but the mind still works in powerful ways.

'Thinking determines your mood, which will lead to a certain type of behaviour, and if you change your thinking, you will change your life.'

He seemed to be at the mercy of his tongue! The words we speak have the ability to change the direction of our thought patterns.

Negative talk is like quicksand - before you know where you are you are sinking.

- "I am an absolute failure."
- "What's the point of living?"
- "I do not like myself or my life."
- "Nothing goes my way."
- "It is always the worst-case scenario for me."
- "Everything is my fault, absolutely everything."

This is a typical rejection scenario:

- So much had been taken away from Mephibosheth.
- He had lost his identity, his family and his inheritance.
- As he grew up he excluded himself by hiding away, as he would have hated probably every aspect of life, including himself and life itself.
- He was extremely fearful so ended up in a place far away, hiding from everyone.
- He was so negative in his thinking and speech. He was angry, bitter and depressed.
- It was as though he had been thrown away and abandoned.
- He was full of guilt and shame (we feel guilty for what we do; we feel shame for who we are).
- All the definitions of rejection, which are rebellion, self-rejection and self-protection, affected him.
- There was such pain in Mephibosheth's heart and he did not have the ability to interpret it. Remember he was only five years old when all of this happened to him.
- When David remembered him, Mephibosheth was probably in his teens so he must have carried these feelings of rejection for at least ten or twelve years.

As you read this consider how this affects you. You may feel that you have lost so much and that all you can do is attempt to ignore the turmoil inside. You do not have to go literally to your Lo-Debar, the land of nothing; the place of no hope, for you can be there in the middle of everyday living. You may not be crippled literally, but you feel helpless with no ability to live in your God given inheritance as His child.

What did Mephibosheth do with rejection? He let it define him and hence control his life. There was no way he could live day by day without showing the effects of rejection. It was there and manifested powerfully in every situation, even when he met King David later (2 Samuel 9:5-8).

Mephibosheth needed deep healing, and the only way was through the kindness of King David (The King's Table chapter deals with the healing of Mephibosheth). The only way for any of us to come into healing is through the kindness of another King.

MEMORY POINTS

- Build on the unfailing love of our heavenly Father.
- God is in search of humanity for love and relationship; God is in pursuit of us.
- Rejection can be a significant threat to our basic human need for stable relationships and how those relationships are worked out.
- Rejection can affect all relationships and every area of a person's life.
- Consider the definitions of rejection and how they can affect your life.
- Rejection will make you feel nobody cares.
- What do we do when rejection comes? Do we let rejection define us and then let it control us? Everyone has been rejected to some degree. It is a big club. Whether rejection defines us or refines us is our choice.
- Remember the innocent five year old who lost everything in a day.
- It is not difficult to dwell in our personal 'Lo-Debars.'

PERCEPTION VS.
TRUTH

We all have challenges regarding who we are and how we should have functional relationships, because we do want to fit in and have good accepting people around us. In a perfect world there would be no rejection but we are not there yet, so how we manage our lives is important to our future.

Our struggle for acceptance will determine how we assess who we are and how we consider the world around us. It is not difficult though, to see everything through the eyes of rejection yet in that there is a conflict because something deep within us wants to see everything through the eyes of acceptance.

We all have a fundamental need to be accepted and to belong. When someone does not feel they belong they strive or perform to be acceptable, which can only make the struggle worse. As we recognise this, we can begin to turn things around with the gracious help of our loving Heavenly Father.

The danger is that a rejected person will probably respond or react in some negative way against the one who has shown rejection. There is a tendency to withdraw on one hand, or fight back on the other. There can be long-term consequences as the struggle to be accepted will root into our lives and sometimes the depth of it will make it difficult to overcome the negative perceptions.

Being rejected in the early years of life can make people highly sensitive to rejection later in life, because the latent pain tends to leak or overflow. This will lead to a further continued negative response and overreaction often tainted with depression. There is a tendency to overthink negative thoughts. Anxiety and even hostility will rise up often with no logical reason.

Those who are less sensitive to rejection can identify more accurately to rejection experiences and respond appropriately.

The challenge in our struggle for acceptance is to get to a consistent loving response. As we follow Jesus, we cannot help see this in all that He did. Acceptance is such a powerful, radical and relational concept. It is more powerful than rejection because love is more powerful. It touches you deep within in such a positive way. Being and feeling accepted and loved will leave no room for rejection. Light can and will overcome darkness, and love will overcome animosity and enmity.

Awareness and understanding of acceptance is good but it is only the first step. We need to consider application. As we begin to devote ourselves to practice this foundational concept, things begin to fall into place. Is it difficult? Yes, because it seems so unnatural to us in our own struggle for acceptance. With the help of the Holy Spirit within us and the love and acceptance of our Father God, we can challenge our mind-set and begin to change.

IDENTITY AND IMAGE

In our consideration of why rejection is a problem, we need to look at some basic areas related to who we are.

It starts with God making an amazing announcement.

'Then God said, "Let us make human beings in our image, to be like ourselves."' Genesis 1:26-27 (NLT).

- We image or reflect God's likeness.
- We have a family resemblance.
- We originate from the Father.
- We are his offspring (Acts 17:28).

Image is a representation; it is a reflection. When God made us in His image, He designed us to be relational beings like Him, capable of touching others in deep ways and of being touched by them. Basically we reflect His life. God literally breathed into us His very life (Genesis 2:7). What a gift! Therefore our identity is rooted in God.

How can we as humans be in God's likeness?

- A mental likeness - an intellectual likeness far superior to any other animal. We have a mind capable of hearing and understanding God's communication, with emotions capable of responding to God in love, and a will to make right choices.
- A moral likeness – a God consciousness or a spirit with an intuitive capacity to know and commune, with an ability to worship and know Him and this includes a capacity to make right choices.
- A social likeness – we are relational, made with a social nature and a need to receive love and to give love. This leads to an intimacy with God. As God said, *"it is not good that man should be alone"* (Genesis 2:18), which can include intimacy with a spouse. We were not made to be alone. We were made to have a caring family and good friends, which bring security and stability to us.

"God saw all that He had made and it was very good" (Genesis 1:31 NIV).

God saw a complete man and woman and was so happy to commune with them in glorious acceptance. God's acceptance clearly affected the way in which the man and the woman saw themselves. This is self-image, which is the overall picture we have of ourselves. It is the way we view ourselves; the thoughts we have of ourselves and the value we place on ourselves.

At the heart of self-image lie our central beliefs, our core values of ourselves. They are statements of fact we have come to learn about ourselves, based on life experiences and messages we have received about the kind of person we are.

Most of our opinions of ourselves would probably not be good, particularly when we feel pressurised by problems and challenges. All around us we are bombarded with voices telling us we need to be better. Maybe the adverts said, "buy this and feel good," or a teacher at school said, "this is not good enough," or our parents who tried to make us do better. All the time there was a nagging feeling that if we could, we would have a little more esteem and value, enough to get us through the day or the difficult period. Of course we never could reach the target and we found ourselves slipping further away believing that nothing will ever change because we could not change.

The message Adam and Eve received was complete and total acceptance, immersed in unconditional love to the point where God Himself came and walked with His children in the garden (Genesis 3:8). It was exquisite harmony, love and trust and a glorious joining of lives. You can't get better than that!

However today things have changed and we see God's likeness defiled and tarnished. We see rejection woven into the core of humanities heart and a negativity that pulls down to destroy. We have been affected and afflicted in every area of image and likeness, mentally, morally and in our social context.

As we will see later, our relationship with our creator God, our loving Heavenly Father, has been severely damaged but not irreparably so, because there is an amazing way out motivated by our Father's love for us. But so many still need to come into the fullness of it.

When our self-esteem is high we feel good about ourselves, we feel in control of our lives, we enjoy the challenges life presents and we know how to make things happen. We are able to make right choices about how to run our lives. However, what rejection does is open us to the opposite – low self-esteem and negativity.

We no longer feel in control of our experiences, so things go out of balance. We do not feel good and rejection is there to feed the negative impulses and will ultimately create a belief system in which we will struggle with acceptance.

The challenge is how we react when we cannot cope. The conflict is that we believe we are made in God's image yet the power of rejection in many cases still has a clear hold on us. We will think our identity and image is in what we do; yet God says our identity is in who we are. The key is not only to remember this but also to live it out, challenging and changing those negative mind-sets.

JABEZ

A book written about Jabez has sold millions around the world (Wilkinson, Bruce. The Prayer of Jabez. Colorado Springs: Multnomah Press, 2000). His mother called him Jabez because he was born in pain! Imagine being called pain! Jabez means to grieve, be sorrowful or trouble, which relates to pain. It could mean he causes sorrow. The scripture says he was more honourable than his brothers (1 Chronicles 4:9). He was recognised for his honourable character, though his mother bore him with sorrow. He was a 'son of sorrow'.

Amidst all of this Jabez had a relationship with God. This relationship was strong and intimate enough to pray a prayer that not only touched the heart of God but also was recorded in scripture, to inspire us to greater things and to overcome our own pain and rejection

Consider His Plight:

1. His name relates to pain and sorrow – not only was Jabez born in pain but also his mother called him a name that related to that pain. She gave him a name that would perpetuate the problem. In that culture it was understood that people and names are intimately related. He could have been a pain maker.

2. He had an ability to cause pain and sorrow – not only was the start of his life difficult but the rest of his life could have been the same, for within him was the ability to hurt himself and others.

3. He came to a great understanding of his past and took responsibility for his pain and became vulnerable. He could have looked at the situation and given up.

Jabez prayed four things:

- That God would bless him indeed.
- That God would enlarge his territory for he wanted to make a mark for God and in society.
- That God's hand might be with him, the hand of blessing, of intimacy and of security.
- That God would keep him from evil. Remember God gives us the right to overcome.

God answered his prayer. His life became a contradiction of his name; the son of pain was free from pain. The consequences of this answered prayer was that Jabez became more honourable than his brothers. The honour was not about personal credit but more of what God thought about him. Honour is the recognition of a person's worth and value, and Jabez reached a place where in his maturity, he surpassed his brothers even though he had such a difficult start.

Honour is all about a good name, esteem, dignity and respect. Even though his circumstances were so difficult, he came through. It was clear that he recognised the problems in his life and even though they were not his fault in the beginning, he took responsibility and by trusting his God pushed through.

The challenge to us is that we can come into the same blessing God gave Jabez. Looking at our beginnings is important. It will affect the way we live, act and behave. Understanding we can do something about the past gives us hope. Even in our rejection all things are possible!

Memory Points

- Rejection is a pain.
- Rejection is pain.
- The pressure of fitting in.
- We are not made to accept the unacceptable.
- Acceptance is such a powerful concept and we can make it a reality.
- We are made in God's likeness.
- Self-image is the picture we have of ourselves.
- Rejection will affect self-image and esteem.
- How do we react when we cannot cope?
- Jabez broke through because of his relationship with God.
- Jabez did not allow the past to control the present or affect the future.

IDENTITY

If you had the opportunity to describe what kind of person you think you are, what would you say? Many people would default to a negative opinion of themselves because of the deeper issues affecting their value and worth. What you believe about yourself will affect the way you live and how you talk and behave.

- Do you think there is something wrong in the way you relate in social interaction?
- Do you believe your self-esteem, value and worth is defined by the approval or disapproval you receive from others?
- Do you believe that you have to please everyone to gain acceptance and approval?
- Do you believe your worth depends on your achievements?
- Do you have to be right about everything to feel good?
- Do you believe that if you look good it will affect your sense of personal value?
- How do you respond when you look in a mirror?
- Do you think you are needed or necessary to what God is doing?
- Do you have a healthy sense of belonging?
- Is there an awareness of being wanted, accepted, cared for, enjoyed and loved?

There is power in the way we think and of course this will influence us in everyday life. Although philosophers have used this statement it was King Solomon who stated, *'As he thinks in his heart so is he'* (Proverbs 23:7). Right or wrong thinking begins with the words we say to ourselves, so every action and feeling is preceded by a thought. *'Life and death are in the power of the tongue'* (Proverbs 18:21). If we become what we think, the challenge is to be cautious about what we allow to fill our minds. What we hold in our minds has an effect on our emotions and even our physical bodies.

BELIEFS AND BEHAVIOUR

Our self-image is formed basically from early childhood by interaction with parental figures, which may be good and positive or the opposite. As children 'we take in well', but do not have the adult ability or experience to interpret or evaluate. The messages received create a belief system, the basis from which we interpret the way we see things. Children do not have the ability or capacity to interpret a new and challenging experience appropriately, which may have repercussions in later life. Some memories will be pleasant, others traumatic, but whether good or bad they help form self-image.

Patterns of thought are established in childhood and they become our way of seeing things, our world-view. For example, if you have been told consistently that you are no-good or useless, this lie will influence your perception of the way you see yourself. This may not be the truth from God's perspective. If you have been hurt through rejection it is not difficult to allow yourself to express ungodly habits, reactions, behaviour and attitudes that can affect the way you see yourself, others and your world-view. It will also affect the way you see God and your perception of how He sees you.

Patterns of behaviour are inherent and recurrent, which result from a trigger, internally or externally releasing the pattern of specific responses. There is a clear sense of rotation or repetition as one specific area of the cycle leads to another. This will be looked at in more detail in the 'Mind Games' chapter.

WHAT KIND OF PERSON WOULD YOU LIKE TO BE?

A confident person with a good self-image, a good sense of value and worth accepted by others, and able to cope daily. Of course, but is it really possible? Look at the following points with an open heart because it is possible for you to attain to all of them. However you feel, whatever you think about yourself, whatever has happened in the past, whatever you have done to yourself or others, it is still possible for you to be this kind of person.

1. To love yourself - You are part of God's creation fearfully and wonderfully made.
2. To understand yourself - Being aware of your strengths and weaknesses, you are able to grow towards maturity.
3. To know what you want - You have and can express confidence in moving forward.
4. To know where you are going - Vision is a word you understand and you are not afraid to set new goals and still live in reality.
5. To think positively - You are not into denial; you do not transfer blame or become overwhelmed by problems.
6. To behave appropriately - You handle each situation you are in with integrity and skill.

This will result in people you relate to feeling:
- Secure because they know where they stand with you. They will not be intimated by you or feel that you are afraid of them.
- Trusted because they know you will not judge, criticise or abuse them.
- Confident because you will encourage them and facilitate them.
- Understood by you and not patronised.
- Not undermined or deceived because you are not perfect and will

acknowledge your own weaknesses and will take responsibility for your actions as and when necessary.

This is the power of acceptance.

It is possible your first response might be "Help! How can I ever get there? It is beyond my ability. I can never do it." You can get there but you may identify with some or all of the following and this is the battleground:

1. I am stupid.
2. I am not worth anything.
3. I am no good.
4. I feel inferior.
5. I will never be able to do it.
6. I am useless.
7. I do not like the way I look.
8. I am a failure.
9. There must be something wrong with me.
10. No one loves me.
11. I am lonely.
12. I want to be like him or her.
13. No one must ever know what I am feeling.

The consequences of these thoughts lead to these fairly obvious conclusions:

- I do not like myself.
- I cannot believe people would like me?
- I do not understand how God can love me?
- I do not know what to do to change all of this.
- I am in conflict because I see the positive but feel trapped in the negative.

How Do I Think God Sees Me?

- What does God see in me?

- How can God value me?
- Who am I to think that God could ever love me?
- I am too bad and God is too big and distant to care about me.

These statements seem huge or even impossible to answer, so we push them into the unconscious part of the mind. The problem is, however, we can never bury these words or our problems dead.

The scripture is crystal clear!

- He loves us (1 John 3:1).
- He is pleased with us (Luke 3:21-22).
- He accepts us (Ephesians 1:6).
- He rejoices over us (Zephaniah 3:17).
- We are his workmanship, the product and result of his skill (Ephesians 2:10).

There are many more scriptures regarding God's love and acceptance. God is good and His love endures, lasts and carries on forever! Our self-esteem then, comes from Him and Him alone and there is nothing that we can do to gain this, there is nothing we can do to earn this.

Satan attacked Jesus through the three temptations in the wilderness. He wanted Jesus to prove Himself, to prove His identity and to prove His calling (Luke 4:1-13). But Jesus had no need to prove anything. God had given Him identity, value and security and that was enough.

As we consider our own trials, temptations and tribulations relating to our identity in God, we can use the words that the Father said to the Son, because they are the same words the Father says to us. In the midst of the accusations and condemnation from the enemy about our identity, we can do what Jesus did and speak out these 'words of God' and live in victory day by day for just as Jesus had nothing to prove neither have we.

WHO DID JESUS SAY HE WAS?

If there was one word that could summarise the Christian Faith, it would probably be relationship. This would be worked out in a relationship with God, which is vertical and relationships with one another, which are horizontal. Our faith then is founded and built on relationships.

Relationship is the place where we see God in Jesus and how we see each other and of course how we see ourselves; the place where acceptance, esteem and value will begin to grow and strengthen our inner lives.

Jesus wanted the disciples not just to understand him or to know about Him, but to know Him. We need God but we also need each other because this will bring understanding and acceptance of who we are.

Today's society is full of conflict in relationships. Everyone longs for relationship but often it is easier to be alone. Intimacy with God causes a true understanding of who we really are and our own sense of value to emerge.

At His baptism Jesus received affirmation from His Father that became foundational in His future ministry. *"You are my Son, whom I love, with you I am pleased"* (Luke 3:21). These words underpinned who He was.

Throughout the gospel of John we read of Jesus declaring who He was. He was not afraid to do this because his sense of esteem and value was right. He knew who He was and nothing could shift Him from that security.

"I AM"

These amazing words show His absolute timeless existence, that He is from eternity to eternity, yet has come into time because of His redemptive love for humanity.

These examples show us the strength of His security in who He was:

- *"I am He"* (John 4:26, the Messiah).
- *"I tell you the truth, before Abraham was born, I Am"* (John 8:58 NIV).
- *"I am the door"* (John 10:9).
- *"I am the good shepherd"* (John 10:11, 14).
- *"I am the resurrection and the life"* (John 11:25).
- *"I am the way, the truth and the life"* (John 14:6).
- *"I am the true vine"* (John 15:1).

Jesus expressed confidently who He was. These are incredible statements. His intimacy with His Father gave Him a true understanding of His worth and value and He knew who He was. In the Old Testament these same words "I Am" have already been used.

When God spoke to Moses about leading the Israelites out of Egypt, Moses said to God, *"if I go to the Israelites and they ask me your name, then what shall I tell them?"* God said to Moses, *"I AM WHO I AM. Say to them: 'I AM has sent you'"* (Exodus 3:13-14). These are the same words Jesus used in the above scriptures.

What was Jesus doing? He was expressing who He was as God in a very confident and secure manner.

When Jesus walked on the water at Galilee towards the disciples' boat and they cried out in fear, He declared something about Himself. He actually responded to them by shouting, "I Am" (Matthew 14:27 literal Greek). He used again the same words that Moses heard.

As they saw the figure through the storm, they thought it was a ghost or a demon from the abyss but it was Jesus walking on the sea. He suspended the laws of gravity by His unlimited power! This was a manifestation of the Godhead, the Lord of nature controlling its powers in sovereign dominion. As Jesus walked on the water He showed His absolute dominance over the perils of the lake.

When God revealed His name to Moses He became a living reality to him and therefore more accessible to him. To know God is to encounter a personal reality. It could mean 'absolute beingness', which is 'is', 'was' and 'always shall be.' God is eternal and immortal, before the beginning and after the end, entirely without limits and the divine name, which declared His character, His attributes and His absolute existence. This is the name Jesus used for Himself.

WHO DO WE SAY WE ARE?

We often use the words "I am" in a negative way:
- "I am no good."
- "I am useless."
- "I am not worth anything."
- "I am rejected."
- "I am a failure."
- "I am finished."

These words are usually unspoken feelings of inadequacy in any challenging situation.

One day as Jesus was speaking to His disciples, He asked them a challenging and intriguing question, one that became crucial in their walk with Him. Jesus asked them to explain who the people thought He was. They said various names but then He asked them directly, *"Who do you say I am?"* Peter had a great revelation, which Jesus rejoiced over; *"You are the Christ, the Son of the living God"* (Matthew 16:13-17). Once we know who He is then we can know who we are. This then will give us the sense of value and worth we desire.

As we get to know Him we can begin to change the way we think and talk.

Here are some positive statements to consider seriously:

- 'I am a new creation' (1 Corinthians 5:17). This is new life in Jesus, which is His life in us.
- 'I am accepted in Christ' (Ephesians 1:6). This is totally unconditional.
- 'I am reconciled to God' (2 Corinthians 5:18). No opposition or judgement from God but joined and united through Jesus.
- "I am now a child of God' (1 John 3:2). This means love and security in His family.
- 'I am free from all condemnation' (Romans 8:1). There is no place for guilt, condemnation or accusation because I have a relationship with Jesus.
- 'I am loved with an everlasting love' (Jeremiah 31:3). Nothing we can do can stop God loving us.
- 'I am chosen to be in Christ' (Ephesians 1:4). We are, by grace, through faith, in Christ continually.

Jesus has made it possible through His life, death and resurrection for us to receive His life, knowing that we can enter into all that He is. His prayer was that we might be one with Him and the Father, *"I in them and you in me"* (John 17:23). We are, as we believe.

How do we really see ourselves? Is it failure, rejection, no sense of value or esteem? Let us begin to understand and accept how God sees us; let us look at ourselves from His perspective because our beginning, end and everything in between is in Him.

The Psalmist writes, *"I am like an olive tree flourishing in the house of God; I trust in Gods unfailing love for ever and ever"* (Psalm 52:8).

This is what to aim for in the way that we think. Please do not struggle to get there. Just receive the fact that God has accomplished it in His Son. We can change our mind-sets by choice, in conjunction with the power of the Holy Spirit working in us.

'Because of Christ's redemption;

I am a new creation of infinite worth,

I am deeply loved,

I am completely forgiven,

I am fully pleasing,

I am totally acceptable to God,

I am absolutely complete in Christ,

There has never been another person like me in the history of mankind,

nor will there ever be,

God has made me an original, one of a kind, a special person!'

This is truth about you and me. *"You will know the truth and the truth will set you free"* (John 8:32).

MEMORY POINTS

- How do you see yourself?
- What do you believe about yourself?
- Do we become what we think?
- What we hold in our mind can affect the rest of our lives.
- Beliefs established in early years can affect lifelong behaviour.
- We can refocus and transform the way we think.
- What kind of person would you like to be?
- How we confess is so vital to our growth in God.
- The power of acceptance is more than we realise but remember, even though there may be a battle we can overcome in Jesus.
- What does God see in you?
- What Jesus has said about Himself gives us the right to say who we are.

IMPACT

Humans are complicated beings! Sketching the human anatomy is relatively straightforward but to understand the soul and spirit of a person is more difficult. There may be some differences in terminology but I would like to go along with the following interpretations, which of course are not definitive. Many years ago my psychiatrist friend said, "the more you narrow the definition, the more difficult the interpretation becomes."

THE MIND

The mind is the element of human consciousness relating to reason, thought, memory, imagination, feeling, will, perception, intellect, understanding and judgement. It is a receptacle, which receives, holds, understands, processes and makes a decision as to what to do in every situation. We saw in the last chapter that the mind affects and influences every part of us. What we hold in our minds has an effect on our emotions. It is not difficult to allow recurrent patterns of behaviour to grow out of what we believe. These can be positive or negative. We need to learn what to do with what we receive, and deal with thoughts of rejection in a positive way for it is not a sin to be tempted. Thoughts of rejection have no place in our lives but the enemy will exploit our vulnerability.

Jesus was so clear when he said, *"these things I have spoken to you, that in Me you may have peace. In the world you will have tribulation; but be of good cheer or take heart, I have overcome the world"* (John 16:33). We will see more of this later but remember who we are in Christ. If He has overcome, so have we. It says we will have tribulation but He gives us peace to face the issues of life.

Quite often things we worry about stay in the mind when we are asleep, and when we wake up they are still there. These thoughts can become obsessive and it is not difficult to speculate, exaggerate or even fantasise about them, but it is rare that any of them actually materialise.

The mind can be simply defined in three areas; the conscious the subconscious and the unconscious. An iceberg is an apt illustration because it is huge and impressive. It is bigger below the surface and the deeper you go the bigger it is. Only a small percentage of the iceberg is visible above the surface.

In the same way we can see how the mind works:

The **conscious** relates to our day-by-day living in this above the surface - in the way we communicate, analyse and evaluate circumstances and events. It is our awareness internally and externally of the present moment. We perceive what happens to us, we make judgements and decisions and we react accordingly.

Just below the surface is the **subconscious** and it seems this area collects, stores and makes accessible information. It is a composition or combination of what is seen and heard that can be retrieved or recalled, as and when necessary by the conscious mind. This could be due to an event or circumstance, which causes a memory to emerge into the consciousness. This part of the mind also seems to be the repository for painful memories not coped with in the conscious area. If they are too hard to live with these memories separate into the unconscious.

The unconscious is an extension of the subconscious; the hidden part of the mind, a reservoir, where belief systems are established that affect the way we consciously think, respond or act. This is the place where our thoughts and memories are out of reach of our conscious mind and we do not have easy access to the information. Throughout childhood many memories and experiences, which are collected and stored, help to mould whom we are today. Although they cannot usually be accessed, they are part of the driving force related to the way we behave.

The unconscious is also an area where repressed and traumatic memories, connected to dissociation or breaking of the personality are hidden. Some have experiences so shocking or traumatizing, that the only way to survive is to detach them from the conscious and push them as far away as possible. These memories cannot be accessed in the same way as those in the subconscious as they are totally buried, but the fact is those memories at whatever depth, are alive, however well hidden - they are still there.

The Apostle Paul gives us great encouragement to think in a positive way and The Message puts it concisely, *"summing it all up, friends, I'd say you'll do best by filling your minds and meditating or thinking on things true, noble, reputable, authentic, compelling, gracious—the best, not the worst; the beautiful, not the ugly; things to praise, not things to curse"* (Philippians 4:18 MESSAGE). The painful memories of rejection can be healed in the authority of the name of Jesus.

THE EMOTIONS

Emotions are feelings. The word is rooted in motion, to set in motion, to excite or disturb. Feelings are moved, stirred or agitated often spontaneously and cause a reaction, mostly through an external experience and then manifest in various ways such as love or hate, joy or sorrow, fear, etc. Emotions can be described as the language of a person's inner self and rejection damages emotions. Obviously people will respond or react differently in a situation according to personality, but we need to remind ourselves suppressing emotions is as hazardous as exploding in anger and pain.

THE SPIRIT

We are spiritual beings with a capacity to perceive and communicate with the supernatural, the invisible world, which is as real as the natural world in which we live. We communicate with the unseen world through our spirit. The spirit is the area of human awareness where man or woman is most sensitive to the spiritual realm. This realm has been called 'the dimension of the beyond in the midst.'

Spirit is basically breath and Job explains it clearly, *"but there is a spirit in man, the breath of the Almighty that gives him life or understanding"* (Job 32:8). Therefore, we are animated or given life from God and that becomes our source of living, centred on its deepest value and meaning. The spirit is the way God most immediately encounters mankind. It is where we are directly open and responsive to God. The scripture brings clarity to this, 'He has also set eternity in the hearts of men' (Ecclesiastes 3:11). If that is so, we can draw near to God and get to know Him through our spirit. As Christians we are taught to live from our spirit where we commune, worship and develop our intuitive nature with God. Since we are much more than an assortment of parts rather an indivisible whole, we need to be aware how one part affects the other. Rejection can affect our spirit, which is vulnerable to wounding.

In the beginning something happened to the spirit of the man and woman, Adam and Eve. When they sinned against God they had to leave the garden and felt desperately rejected. Remember God breathed into man the breath of life and he became a living being or soul (Genesis 2:7). There is then something immortal and eternal about us and it is this area, which can be affected.

'A merry heart makes a cheerful countenance, but by sorrow of the heart the spirit is broken' (Proverbs 15:13). *'A merry heart does good, like medicine, but a broken spirit dries the bones'* (Proverbs 17:22). *'A man's spirit sustains him in sickness but a crushed or wounded spirit who can bear'* (Proverbs 18:14 NIV).

THE HEART

It seems that frequently the word heart and spirit are used in an interchangeable way in scripture. Does that mean they are the same? If the spirit is the core of the soul (emotions and mind) there is separateness but an obvious connection, which is unity. The heart by definition is the central part of our being, which includes the body and again you cannot divide each area and define, because each is in union and humanity cannot exist without the harmony and blending of each one.

This is a mystery, which can be explored but not exhausted. We know from experience that God by His Spirit dwells in the depths of our being whether it be heart or spirit. Scripture is clear that the heart can be broken but it also underlines the fact that the broken heart can be healed.

- *'He heals the broken-hearted and binds up their wounds'* (Psalm 147:3).
- *"The Spirit of the Lord God is upon me, because the Lord has anointed me to preach good tidings to the poor; He has sent me to heal the broken-hearted, to proclaim liberty to the captives, and the opening of the prison to those who are bound"* (Isaiah 61:1).
- *"He has sent me to heal the broken-hearted"* (Luke 4:18).

There Is Hope.

"For there is hope for a tree, if it is cut down, that it will sprout again, and that its tender shoots will not cease. Though its root may grow old in the

earth, and its stump may die in the ground, yet at the scent of water it will bud and bring forth branches like a plant." (Job 14:7-9). So many of us can identify with Job's cry. There is hope for a tree ravaged by the destruction of rejection. Water, the very life and spirit of our God, is the source of our restoration!

THE BODY

It is probable that internalising in all or any of the above areas can affect the body. If there has been stress from rejection, psychosomatic (mind to body) illnesses can develop. It is possible to have stress headaches, suffer depression and feel exhausted; aches and pains appear in your body through consistently feeling emotionally overwhelmed. You may become anxious and fearful about the future: you feel, hopeless and helpless.

Later we will discuss the many causes of rejection and how inner and physical healing can take place in the name of Jesus releasing us from the power and roots of rejection.

MEMORY POINTS

- We are complicated beings so be careful how you define soul and spirit because it will affect your interpretation.
- The mind is a receptacle, which receives, processes and makes decisions.
- What we hold in our minds will affect our emotions.
- Remember the iceberg.
- Emotions are the language of our inner self.
- Emotions can be expressed, suppressed or repressed.
- We touch the unseen, the supernatural, through our spirit.
- The spirit is the breath of God within us, giving us an ability to communicate with Him.
- Rejection can crush or wound our spirit.

- The heart is the centre of who we are and is in unity with the mind, emotions and spirit.
- The heart can be broken.
- The body can be made sick by the stress of internal pain.
- Jesus declared He can and will heal the broken-hearted.

OPPOSITION

As we look at rejection, it is vital we consider the fact that Satan and his demonic powers will use, indiscriminately, rejection to undermine our relationship with God, how we see ourselves and how we live our lives.

Jesus referred to the Devil as 'the prince of this world' (John 12:31). When the disciples asked Jesus to teach them to pray, one of the petitions was, "deliver us from the evil one" (Matthew 6:13). He warned them to "watch and pray so that you will not fall into temptation" (Mark 14:38 NIV). This was at the time when Jesus went through an agonising time of temptation at Gethsemane just before His death. Not only was Jesus tempted just before the end of his life, but was also tempted right at the beginning of His ministry in the wilderness, when the Devil came three times and attempted to draw Jesus away from His destiny (Luke 4:2). Many times in his ministry there were confrontations with the enemy regarding setting people free from all sorts of oppression (Luke 13:16). He even stilled a storm on Lake Galilee by rebuking the wind and the waves in a language that was normally used for dealing with demons (Mark 4:39).

Please bear in mind the risk we take if we either ignore the enemy or be obsessive in his involvement with us. It is clear there are other reasons for our difficulties than just his involvement, such as the sinfulness of humanity in a fallen world. We all know we can act irresponsibility, which is our choice.

Some people exaggerate the Devil's influence believing that all problems whether physical, emotional, mental or social always have a demonic source. On the other hand, it is unwise to disregard the Devil and then blame God or other people when things go wrong.

"There are two equal and opposite errors into which our race can fall about the devils (demons). One is to disbelieve their existence. The other is to believe, and to feel an excessive and unhealthy interest in them" (Lewis, C. S. The Screwtape Letters. Glasgow: Collins, 2012).

As we have in our humanity, an ability through our spirits to touch the invisible or the supernatural, we need to be very aware of what is there and how we perceive, understand and handle it.

Scripture talks about a war, a conflict between Satan and God and we are caught up in it as supernatural powers attack, oppress and attempt to affect us. *"This is no afternoon athletic contest that we'll walk away from and forget about in a couple of hours. This is for keeps, a life-or-death fight to the finish against the Devil and all his demonic angels"* (Ephesians 6:12 MESSAGE). We understand this scripture as not wrestling against flesh and blood but against powers in the spiritual realm. The battle is real, demonic power is real and they will do all they can to hinder, harass and even try to bring destruction. The power of rejection is a strong tool in the armoury of the enemy.

As my friend Eric Delve says, "Satan hates God. Humans are made in God's image. They remind him of God - so he hates you. By attacking the body and mind, the heart and wrecking the psychology, he continually tries to ruin God's beautiful masterpiece" (Delve, Eric. To Boldly Go. Echoes in Eternity, 2013).

WORLD-VIEW

This basically means how we see and interpret the world with reference to our own collection of beliefs about it. It is the way we think about the world.

What is our world-view regarding the supernatural and how does that affect us from a Christian standpoint, when considering how the supernatural affects us. We are dealing with the invisible world and basically cannot see what is going on. We do not like to touch that which we do not understand or cannot see so Western mind-sets are disturbed. We have a spirituality that can discern the invisible to the point where occasionally angels and demons can be sensed or even seen. We have the ability to discern, which is to distinguish, to detect or even recognise the invisible powers.

It is possible we have been affected in two ways:

Firstly, by the problem of a rationalistic, scientific world-view that assumes there is no reality beyond the natural and that there is only a material universe. This affects us all in one way or another probably through fear or unbelief. It is easier to have this more Western mind-set, where the mind has the throne and is saviour. Someone has said, "It is ignorance, not Satan, we are to fight."

Second, is the belief that everything has two opposite and equal parts. Some would say the universe is under the dominion of two opposing principles, one good and the other evil. There is a clear assumption of the existence of a spirit world. It is such a major theme in scripture highlighted by the clash of two kingdoms. God and Satan however are not in a mighty cosmic conflict of the 'Luke Skywalker and the evil Darth Vadar'. It is not an equal and opposite spiritual struggle. We do need to remember who God is and that He created Satan and that He is infinitely greater than him. He is the dominant power in the universe. The truth is Satan has some power but he is no equal to God and that evil is a lesser force already defeated through Jesus.

Summary

- We are spiritual beings that can touch a spiritual world.
- We are in a battle and demonic forces can affect and harass us.
- We remind Satan of God because we are in His image therefore we are targets of Satan's rebellion and hatred.
- Many have been affected by a flawed worldview undermining our walk of faith.
- Perhaps more education is necessary on the various aspects of the supernatural especially Satan and the demonic powers.
- We are not caught up in an equal and opposite universal battle.

CAN DEMONS AFFECT REJECTED PEOPLE?

Satan The Accuser

The name Satan means 'accuser' or 'adversary' (Revelation 12:10). There are incidents in scripture where the 'enemy' would accuse, but Jesus brings clarity to the situation as he declares Satan is the 'father of lies' (John 8:44). So the accusations of Satan are consistent with who or what he is, the personification of evil. Someone has said that when Satan reminds you of your past remind him of his future. The key for us is to learn to recognise the accuser and then do something about it. His way is deceptive and subtle and will use our mind to make us think we are what he says. He will do what he can to stop us believing that God actually accepts us. We need to remember where these thoughts of rejection have come from or we may find we become fearful and we begin to believe the lies. The enemy will make us think we are saying these things to ourselves, when the reality of the deception is that he is doing it.

The scripture clearly states, *'as he thinks in his heart, so is he'* (Proverbs 23:7). How we think is crucial and rejection does get to the very root of who we are and will undermine our perception of our identity and image. If we take on negative thoughts, the time will come when we will begin to feel worthless, useless, inadequate and inferior. We know that is not right but we still think and act in a way that is the opposite to what we know the Christian life is. We learn to hide our true feelings and do what we think people expect. We try to impress in our struggle to overcome the feelings of rejection, because we long for acceptance.

Are the Devil and the demonic powers behind this? They will attack our weak areas and attempt to make us ineffective.

Demonic Powers

Rejection can violate a person with all kinds of hurts and wounds to the point where character, personality and even the heart and spirit are affected, causing problems in the emotions, the mind and sometimes the body. It is clear that the demonic can use these wounds and hurts to gain entrance. Demons have no respect for rejected and broken people and will take every advantage to afflict, oppress and create bondage. It has been said, "the enemy has one main objective; to prevent us from serving Christ effectively."

CAN CHRISTIANS HAVE DEMONS?

The subject of Christians and demons is full of controversy. We have seen many Christians who find themselves oppressed in some way. There is no doubt that the power of rejection will give access to evil spirits. They can attach themselves to a particular wound or hurt and begin to create bondage. Hurts and wounds need to be healed but demonic bondages need to be broken.

The vast majority of demonised Christians are already demonised when they come to Christ. They have experienced a change of ruler in their spirit but have not attained complete freedom. A demon cannot live in a Christian's spirit because Jesus lives there, but they can live in other parts just as sin can.

Demons cannot indwell a Christian in the same way the Holy Spirit does. A demon never rightfully or permanently dwells in a Christian as the Holy Spirit does. The Holy Spirit enters by uniting with the spirit or heart as the person surrenders to Christ. That part of the Christian becomes alive with the Spirit of Christ and the demonic cannot invade that area. Demons can, however, live in the believer's mind, emotions or body.

The key is a transfer of power and ownership. As we begin to take ground in our own lives and as we begin to grow in Christ, problems will come because power encounters will happen. Our authority over demons is derived solely from the fact that Jesus won the victory over Satan at the cross by His shed blood, death and resurrection. *"Do not give the devil a foothold, an opportunity, a place or location"* (Ephesians 4:27 NIV). So as much as the enemy is able to entice, harass, defile, deceive etc, we have an authority in Christ that, when exercised in the right way, will stop him having his way in our lives. We need to be aware that Christians are not immune to the attacks of the enemy.

As we know 'the flesh' describes our basic nature, which is opposed to the spirit (Galatians 5:19-21). Not all works of the flesh are demons, but sometimes demons can oppress because of the works of the flesh. The Christian has two enemies, the flesh and the demonic and the mind is indeed the battlefield.

Demons are spirit beings and need minds, emotions or bodies through which to express themselves. The issue is not possession it is yielding. We know that temptation can lead to sin through choice (James 1:14).

We yield to temptation through choice; this leads to sin, we either chose to repent or to sin again. As we practise sin we will move into habit and finally bondage, which allows the demonic to take control in that particular area. *'A person without self-control is like a city whose walls are broken down'* (Proverbs 25:28 NIV). The demonic will invade but this is not possession or ownership. The word in the original language is 'diamonizomai' meaning to be demonized in a particular area in your life. If they have a legal right, demons can have access to anyone Christian or not.

We need to know that through the cross the penalty of sin and the power to sin was broken. If we are a new creation (2 Corinthians 5:17) and the old has passed away, surely we are dead to sin and to the power of the flesh (Romans 6:2). Our old self was crucified to sin and we are no longer slaves to sin (Romans 6:6). What do we do and how do we live? We count ourselves dead to sin and we do not let sin reign (Romans 6:11-12). Do we have to sin? Do we need to? Surely if we are dead to it we have the power of the Holy Spirit to overcome. Dead people do not sin...do they?

A Man Affected By Demons

There is much in the gospels about Jesus dealing with the demonic powers that affect people and one incident although quite extreme can help us understand some of the principles of rejection (Mark 5:1-20). This man was clearly demonised and we need to realise that demonic powers will affect someone with rejection. He lived in the cemetery among the graves and tombs and could not be restrained. Night and day he roamed through the graves and cried out loudly, mutilating himself.

In principle the power of rejection is similar:

- There is a tendency for a rejected person to feel they are never fully alive and any relationship with God is compromised.

- It is not difficult for a rejected person to feel out of control in the mind and emotions.
- This is not a one-off issue; it is continuous and will surface consistently as circumstances dictate.
- The emotional pain can be explosive if triggered by any situation at almost any time, which can be very damaging.
- Rejection will attempt to make you hurt yourself with your own pronouncements or curses or even by self-harming.
- People with rejection find it easy to hurt other people with words or behaviour.

The drama of the man amongst the graves is quite extreme. Rejected people may not be running around naked, but they have known a stripping away inside and it is as though identity, destiny and the ability to live a full life has been stolen. Yet even though the enemy has come to steal, kill and destroy, Jesus has come to give us life with abundance (John 10:10).

It is incredible to me that a man in that state would see Jesus quite a distance away and run as fast as he could to him. Surely the demonic powers who knew who Jesus was would want to make the man run in the opposite direction. Even in his greatest need the man still had the will to seek Jesus. He fell on his knees and submitted to Jesus. Be challenged and make those right choices and come to Jesus.

Jesus knew who the demons were and recognised their power to afflict people and was able to do something about it. Jesus began His ministry with a declaration of the kingdom of God. It was a new age, a new realm, a new beginning and He went about restoring lives, healing the sick and dealing with demonic bondage. He said, *"if I cast out demons by the Spirit of God, surely the kingdom of God has come upon you"* (Matthew 12:28).

The kingdom of God is here among us and in Jesus' name we can know a freedom and liberty from the power of rejection.

MEMORY POINTS

- We have an innate ability to touch the supernatural.
- We are in a war, the battle is real and the demonic powers are real.
- Demonic powers can affect us in various ways.
- Our world-view is crucial as to how we see and understand the supernatural.
- Demons affect rejected people and demons affect Christians.
- The key is power and ownership.
- Jesus has the power and authority to deal with demonic powers.
- He has given us the same power and authority through the Holy Spirit.
- We have the ability to make right choices.
- Therefore Jesus is able to free us from the power of rejection and its consequences.

GENERATIONAL INHERITANCE

Heredity is the passing on of physical or mental characteristics, genetically, from one generation to another. Our childhood is shaped by our parents' way of life and the way they conduct themselves. Their view of life, as the cup being half-full or half-empty, will direct the child to the road toward optimism or pessimism. We inherit personality, character, behaviour and all sorts of qualities and physicalities from our parents and maybe even our ancestors. We have both individual and also family characteristics. Some exist from birth, others are learned behaviour. How often have you heard, "you really look like your mum or dad," "you speak just like your mum or dad." We are grateful for all of the good family traits but recognise they may not all be good.

It is possible to inherit negative effects and curses through generational and ancestral ties. This can be described as a spiritual bondage that is passed down from one generation to another where demonic powers are involved. Symptoms of generational curses are continual negative patterns repeated from generation to generation. Although we can exhibit the same behaviour as our parents we need to know that all that Jesus did at the cross has the power to set us free from any of the negative traits inherited. The power of rejection can be inherited through the family.

Scripture is clear on two points:

1. God can visit the sins of the fathers on the sons and daughters. We can inherit sin and every kind of weakness to the third and fourth generations (Exodus 20:3-5, 34:5-7). Even the whole issue of illegitimacy is referred to in this manner but for ten generations (Deuteronomy 23:2).

Cain the firstborn of Adam and Eve is the first example of hereditary rejection shown in his hurts, insecurity, anger, depression, utter selfishness, arrogance, rebellion and ultimately murder (Genesis 4:1-14). *'Our fathers sinned and are no more, but we bear their iniquities'* (Lamentations 5:7).

Peter talks about us, *'being redeemed from the empty way of life handed down to you from your forefathers with the precious blood of Christ'* (1 Peter 1:18-19 NIV). This speaks about something handed down from the forefathers and that wasn't good.

2. The power of the cross deals with any and every generational issue. Even in the old covenant God said, *"the fathers eat sour grapes and the children's teeth are set on edge"* (Ezekiel 18:2). He added, *"don't say that proverb any more for every living soul belongs to Me"* (Ezekiel 18:3-4). We have been freed to walk in the spirit in a personal relationship with God and not in the futility or the ineffectiveness of life as others do (Ephesians 4:17). The past has been dealt with and we have come into an inheritance that can never perish, spoil or fade, because it is shielded by God's power (1 Peter 1:3-5 NIV).

Moses declared to the Lord that He is slow to anger abounding in love and forgiving sin and rebellion, yet He does not leave the guilty unpunished even to the third and fourth generation and asked the Lord to forgive and pardon the children of Israel and He did (Numbers 14:18-20). This tells us to look ahead to Jesus and the ultimate sacrifice for past, present and future sins.

There is a contention that generational curses have been dealt with at the cross, that every past issue has been dealt with and the past has been wiped clean by the death of Jesus. It is true that the cross has broken the power of sin and the power to sin; everything has been dealt with and we now have the ability in Jesus, by the power of the Holy Spirit, to overcome what the past throws up. This is not a magical event that wipes everything away, but more a glorious happening that gives us the ability, by faith, to live in the power of God and not be controlled by the past. We need to learn to possess our possessions or inheritance (Obadiah 17) or in other words, understand, realise and take on board the fact that God has given us everything - and then learn to live knowing that and be overcomers. It is true to say that the judgement of God to visit the sins on the generations is no longer applicable, for we live in the favourable (grace) year of the Lord. At the beginning of His ministry, when Jesus quoted from the book of Isaiah in the synagogue at Nazareth, He deliberately stopped reading just before the verses about God's judgement (Luke 4:17-21). We are in an era of grace. However it is up to us to choose to live in it.

In the light of this there is a further important point to consider. 'The sins of parents create a predisposition, not a destiny' (Leaf, Caroline. Switch On your Brain. Grand Rapids: Baker, 2013). Predisposition is having a tendency or bias to react or behave in a particular way, influenced by past generations. We do not have to behave like they did. We are not responsible for their behaviour and we can make a decision to have nothing to do with it. Our responsibility comes in understanding and acknowledging the sin and making right choices, by understanding and choosing to eradicate it. We can apply the work of the cross to our lives, with repentance and confession and deal with any negative predisposition. Why should we have a bias towards something negative that we see in our family line?

Once we recognise this, we can do something about it because we have the ability through the power of Jesus' name to remove these things from our lives. There may be some demonic activity but we know the reason the Son of God appeared was to destroy the devil's work (1 John 3:8). Why should we agree to the sins of the fathers undermining our God given destiny?

Remember, *'there is now no condemnation for those who are in Christ Jesus'* (Romans 8:1). We are not condemned, we are not guilty; we have been set free through the shed blood of Jesus. *'Jesus gave Himself for us to redeem us from all wickedness and to purify for Himself a people that are His very own'* (Titus 2:13-14 NIV).

'Christ has redeemed us from the curse of the law, having become a curse for us (for it is written, cursed is everyone who hangs on a tree), that the blessing of Abraham might come upon the Gentiles in Christ Jesus, that we might receive the promise of the Spirit through faith' (Galatians 3:13-14).

Any curse from the past is broken, it has lost its power and once we recognize what those curses are in our lives we can in Jesus' name take steps to walk in freedom.

People who are not Christians and Christians who are not free are probably not aware of the fact we can be set free from the control of the past. Even though we are Christians, we may not know or realise what Jesus has done for us. When people become Christians, they can be helped to understand and walk in the liberty that Jesus has given us. Have we dealt with the legal rights the enemy might have in our lives? Something like unforgiveness that affects us because of neglect, abandonment and rejection, gives the enemy rights to control these areas.

Evil spirits are able to affect people ancestrally, because there is a connection through the spiritual ties in family and also other meaningful relationships. Generational spirits are real and they are able to pass down the generation line. They are sometimes called 'familial spirits' or 'ancestral spirits.' The person would have the same struggles their parents had. Any demonic power can be dealt with in Jesus' name. We have no need to fear the past for we can push through into our future destiny in Jesus.

PERSONAL RESPONSIBILITY

Although our ancestors' sins have affected us, we are also held accountable by God for our own sin and behaviour. We cannot shift the blame. We can make right choices and take responsibility. We are affected by our parents' sins for their sins become our sins. However, God has provided the way for our freedom from all the effects of their sin as well as our own. We cannot or should not blame someone else for our troubles, or have an unhealthy obsession with the past but consider these issues with reality and humility.

SOUL TIES

The Bible does not use the word soul tie, but it speaks of them when it talks about souls being knit together, becoming one flesh. A soul tie can serve many functions, but in its simplest form, it ties two souls together in the spiritual realm.

Wrong emotional ties and wrong bonding can affect relationships especially in families. There may be other people such as those that have influenced us throughout the years such as friends, teachers or bosses. Bonds or soul ties hold us in relationship with people.

Godly ties are formed through loving and caring relationship, whether in family or in a strong friendship such as David and Jonathan (1 Samuel 18:1-4).

Ungodly ties are formed through unhealthy relationships with those who wish to dominate, control or abuse mentally, sexually or physically. There are many negative consequences, which will even affect the health of the body.

It needs to be underlined that people can be controlled, manipulated or dominated against their will, even as children. Look at this in the context of family regarding the power of rejection:

Domination by a mother figure could be defined as a matriarchal spirit. The way this can affect men is to cause insecurity and they tend to be ruled by their emotions, behaving like little boys even into adulthood. The scripture implies a man leaves but a woman is given (Genesis 2:24). Sometimes this does not happen for the tie to parents is too strong to allow it.

Domination by a wife can be expressed in sexual control and/or emotional manipulation, which can be subtle.

Domination by a husband, who controls in all domestic and personal ways creating in his spouse a feeling of worthlessness. This will bring a fear of rejection and self-rejection with the accompanying hurts, bitterness, hate, and anger often hidden as in abusive relationships.

Domination by a father can be harsh, unemotional, unreal, religious, legalistic, always right, exceedingly controlling and showing no love or affection.

Domination and control of children can give a perception of not being loved. A rejected person may have a home but feel homeless and doesn't feel at home anywhere. He or she is afraid to trust, to open their heart to receive love and cannot give love or unconditionally express or receive love.

All this will show itself in some kind of rejection, whether a fear of rejection so that you self-protect or perform to gain acceptance or self-rejection whereby you reject yourself or become angry.

GENERATIONAL BLESSING

This term is not found in the scripture, but there are clear indications that positive blessings were given. To bless means basically to invoke, summon or bestow divine favour.

We are the seed of Abraham and therefore come into the blessings that God declared to him. The Lord said to Abraham, *"in you shall all the families of the earth be blessed"* (Genesis 12:1-2, 22:15-18, 26:1-5). This is repeated three times emphasising its importance. It is as though God repeats Himself to ensure we receive His words.

To underline this Peter repeats the promise as he speaks to the gathered people in Jerusalem at Pentecost. He emphasises that through Jesus God will bless us and turn every one of us away from our iniquities (Acts 3:25-26). This is beyond comprehension but it shows the heart of our God.

Often we tend to emphasise the wrong thing; so when we look at generational iniquity we all know that scripture talks about the sins of the fathers affecting the third and fourth generations, but we fail to appreciate that our Father God shows his love to a thousand generations (Exodus 20:6 NIV). We could interpret that as eternity. I would rather dwell on a thousand generations of acceptance than three or four of rejection! This promise is repeated and, as usual, there are conditions. The scripture declares that God is faithful to us and will keep his covenant of love with us to a thousand generations, as we love him and keep His commandments (Deuteronomy 7:9).

The Psalms highlight this fantastic promise, *"He remembers His covenant forever, the word He commanded for a thousand generations the covenant He made with Abraham"* (Psalm 105:8-9). I want to bless any of you affected by the power of rejection and all that it means with the prayer of blessing that the Lord gave Moses to give to the people. *"The Lord bless you and keep you; The Lord make His face to shine upon you, and be gracious to you. The Lord lift up His countenance on you, and give you peace"* (Numbers 6:24-27). Remember too that after the prayer the Lord then said, "this prayer puts My name on the people." We have His name on us. Not the name rejection but the name of our loving heavenly Father.

FIVE GENERATIONS

An illustration of generational curses and blessing can be seen in my own family line, stretching back five generations to the beginning of the First World War. This is my family line on my father's side from my grandfather, my father, me (third generation), our two daughters, the fifth generation our three grandchildren.

The story starts with a young man born in 1892. He married in 1913 and went to the great war of 1914 - 1918 where he saw its horror at close hand with men killed on each side of him. He survived and was awarded the Military Medal for valour. On his return although he was physically fine he was deeply hurt inside, angry, frustrated and disappointed. He returned to a despairing wife who was wondering whether she would ever see her husband again. There was no social networking, mobile phone or e-mail.

We need to realise the terrible consequences that affected families from this war. The men who went to war would have been devastated emotionally, mentally, physically and spiritually. Imagine no contact except the fear of receiving a telegram telling you your husband had been killed. My grandfather came home apparently well, but inside him was a morass of shock, trauma, anger, fear and pain. He, along with most soldiers, would not talk about the experience. Couples had to start relating again. The pain lay dormant.

There must have been thoughts or even fears about how the homecoming soldiers would fit back into family life, particularly with the massive internal change war had made. Remember there was never any war like the First World War. Would my grandmother, who would have felt alone and abandoned for those years, accept him? He had changed; he carried memories he could not express.

My grandparents had more babies. There were probably five or six over the same number of years. Life was hard but they managed. Two of the children died in their early years. A generation of young men and women were affected by the war and so were their children.

By 1939 one of the sons, my father, was about nineteen years old. The pain and anger of my grandfather had passed to him. He joined the army and was sent away as the Second World War began. He was still in the UK so could visit home fairly easily. It was considered the First War was the war to end all wars but another one shook a vulnerable and fragile world. Men who had gone through the First War now found themselves caught up in another conflict. Sons born at the end of the First War were also involved. The pain of the First flowed to the Second. Generational anger and fear was inherited, which brought rejection rather than peace, love and acceptance.

Life was cheap, for who knows what the next day might bring! I remember my mother telling me how they hid under the dining table as the bombs rained down. This affected relationships, and many married young women saw their husbands go to war, either never to see them again or see them return four or five years later. During that time babies were born and they may have been up to five years old before Dad even knew they existed. So life was lived a day at a time; relationships were not permanent and illegitimate children were born. Later, when soldiers came from North America, the problem grew as lonely young women became pregnant. When the invasion of Europe happened, the soldiers were gone and the children born as a result of this never knew their fathers.

The memories of those days were embedded into the hearts of those who experienced the horror of war. The pain affected the children too, as they experienced rejection instead of acceptance. This may have been unintentional but was still very real. Many children, who were born in or at the end of the Second War, were born out of dysfunctional relationships such as:

- Not ever knowing their father. Maybe they were European or North American.

- Growing up without the nurture of a father.
- A woman, although married to a man she had not seen for some years becomes pregnant with someone else.
- Threatened abortion or adoption.
- Living in families where everyone knew someone who was killed fighting or killed because their homes were bombed.
- Living with a tremendous fear of the future.
- The intense, quite unbearable emotional, mental and spiritual pain of war.
- Women had to take responsibility because most of the men had gone to war.
- A father returning home after the war not knowing how to relate to his child.
- A child confused about how to relate to a stranger called 'Dad.'

I was the third generation and was born at the end of the Second War. I was predisposed to pain and anger because of the experiences of my grandfather and father. There was so much missing in those early years, but what I remember most is the lack of affection, which added to the power of rejection in my life. There were many children like me at the time in many nations of the world. There still are because war continues to create that kind of pain.

Many children in my generation were brought up without the communication of love. It took a long time to get back to a sort of normality, but things were never the same. Sometimes a child's circumstances of birth were hidden but that gave rise to problems later when things came to light. You cannot blame those who did not wish to speak about the problems of war but neither can you bury these issues dead.

The effects of war can undermine and even destroy any response to God. Something spiritual happens, whereby the new generation and those following find the concept of God, as a loving Heavenly Father, so difficult to perceive - so church becomes irrelevant.

The pain and hurt passed through the generations and the consequence was more rejected people. The key change for me was embracing Christianity in 1965. That opened a door for a process of healing to take place, leading me from the pain of rejection into the Father's love.

The fourth generation: our daughters were born in the 1970's and one of the first things we did as parents was to declare that we would love our children unconditionally giving them value, esteem and acceptance. Since then nothing has changed and we continue to do this regardless of age.

The fifth generation from the First War is now with us and we have grandchildren. They are very secure in the unconditional love of their families. They are utterly accepted and this is foundational in their characters and personalities. Acceptance is a key in their identity and will be so in their destiny.

MEMORY POINTS

- As much as there are generational curses, we need to underline the fact that there is generational blessing.
- We are not destined to live with our families' sins.
- We inherit good/bad and positive/negative traits from our families.
- Bonds or soul ties hold us in relationship with people; they can be Godly or ungodly.
- Spiritual bondage can also be passed through the generations.
- The power of the cross has dealt with the bondage. We can and need to act on the freedom offered.
- Personal responsibility and making right choices are vital in the process.
- We can know freedom from rejection and live in the acceptance and unconditional love of our Heavenly Father.

THE GOOD SHEPHERD

Have you ever seen a sheep in a field on its back with its legs in the air? Without help the sheep will not be able to get up. It will die. A sheep on its back reminds me of rejected people, because there is a sense of helplessness and hopelessness, with no strength, ability or even the desire to get up.

Jesus called himself the Good Shepherd (John 10:11). When He said this He was saying something very significant. He told us He is the Good Shepherd. Does that mean there are shepherds who are not good?

Many rejected people have trusted their lives to, listened to, submitted to and responded to those they thought were good shepherds, but who have turned out not to be so good. I am not just talking about those in church situations who are leaders, but someone who guides, directs and nurtures in any context such as home, family, school, the place of work and also those close friends to whom we would be vulnerable. We look for good shepherds and sometimes find ourselves wounded by those we have really trusted. The Good Shepherd gives us hope in our rejection.

David became a shepherd and wrote about it in Psalm 23.

Caring and tending the sheep gave David a love for people. God brought him from tending the sheep to be the shepherd of his people. *'He shepherded them with integrity (reliability, honesty, honour) of heart and with skilful hands he led them'* (Psalm 78:71-72). David was a kind man (2 Samuel 9:3) showing his kindness when he gave Mephibosheth a home. Jesus was and is a kind, caring and Good Shepherd.

A shepherd in biblical times tended his flock day and night. He would gather the sheep into a sheepfold at night for their protection. The sheepfold was a pen, a cave, or an area backed by a stone wall. The shepherd would often sleep or sit in the entrance of the sheepfold, ready to guard his sheep from harm. He loved and shielded them and, if necessary, he would lay down his life for them. He would have to locate good pasture, and find quiet pools of water, because sheep will not drink from a fast-flowing river. He had to protect the flock against attack by wolves or other predators. He was responsible for keeping the sheep clean, in good health and making them feel safe. The shepherd had to be constantly alert to the state of his flock for possible dangers or disturbances. In the same way Jesus the Good Shepherd has given Himself by laying down His life for each one of us.

WHO IS MY SHEPHERD?

Psalm 23 beautifully highlights David's response to the Good Shepherd. Consider this psalm in the light of our own rejection.

v1, The Lord is my Shepherd
It starts with God as Lord. Lord means master. We may be sheep, but we are also servants. This is so personal. We can have a relationship with God where we can say, "He is my Shepherd!'" When Jesus said, 'I am the Good Shepherd' He was saying He is our Good Shepherd as He is David's. We belong to Him. David is expressing relationship, which means closeness and intimacy.

"I am the Good Shepherd; I know My sheep and My sheep know Me" (John 10:14 NIV). The shepherd goes ahead of them and his sheep follow him because they know his voice. He knows us and we can know Him, then we can follow Him because we know His voice (John 10:4). This brings safety and security. The shepherd knows every sheep personally although they probably all look the same to us. Sheep will stay close to a good shepherd. A good shepherd is alert and responsible for the total welfare of the sheep. An experienced shepherd knows the names, habits, the condition and health of all his sheep, maybe two thousand of them! Actually each one bleats differently. Sheep do not take care of themselves, they require more attention and care than any other animal.

v1, *I shall not want*
This is provision. Another definition is being contented and peaceful in the shepherd's care. He delights in his flock and is selfless in his response to them. Remember though, he provides what he thinks they need not what they think they want.

v2, *He makes me lie down in green pastures*
If He thinks we need to, He will make us lie down not in scrubby, brown, barren fields but in lush, green pastures because to rest, the sheep must be free from fear and tension. It makes sense that sheep will become quiet, comfortable and secure when they see the shepherd in the field. Green pastures do not come by chance either. Preparation means hard work for the shepherd. He has to dispose of all sorts of stones, roots and rubbish.

v2, *He leads me by still waters*
When sheep become thirsty they become restless. It is very much like how rejected people thirst for acceptance. We find living water by finding Him. Our cry is for refreshment and satisfaction and He calls us to drink from Him, *"if anyone thirsts let him come unto me and drink"* (John 7:37-39).

v3, *He leads me in paths of righteousness for His name's sake*
Sheep are creatures of habit and they will always use the same path. Habitual paths will bring poverty and disaster if the land is overgrazed. Breaking habits is the key to release but rejected people often get stuck where they are. They get entangled in the cycle of specific and habitual mind-sets and they get nowhere. They want to be lead into fresh pasture but feel blocked, even when they know there is a way forward.

v4, *though I walk through the valley of the shadow of death, I will fear no evil; for you are with me; your rod and your staff, they comfort me*
This speaks of danger yet there is a way through as the shepherd guides the sheep to the way out. It is necessary to go through the valley where the grass grows best, as it is the route to the high country, the mountains. The Good Shepherd says He is the way (John 14:6). We do not stay in the valley we walk through without rushing or being fearful. He gives us strength through His perfect love, which deals with the fear (1 John 4:18). He is with me. His rod and staff will comfort and protect but not abuse. We have the Comforter the Holy Spirit, with us and in us.

v5, *you prepare a table before me in the presence of my enemies*
For sheep this could be flat pasture right up in the mountain area, prepared and waiting for the sheep to arrive in the summer. For us, the Lord provides a table right in the presence of our enemies where He can sit and eat with us. A meal expresses a bond of friendship and covenant. Moses took the elders up the mountain to see God and they did what was natural; they ate and drank as a sign of relationship, of family (Exodus 24:9-11).

Jesus wanted to come into the church at Laodicea and eat with the people but they left Him outside (Revelation 3:20). To eat speaks of closeness, intimacy, openness and family. This is the security we have because He is with us even in the presence of our enemies. What security! There were wild and ferocious animals inhabiting those high areas, such as the mountain lion, the bear and the wolf. That is more than enough to bring fear but the shepherd always protected his sheep.

v5, *You anoint my head with oil*
This type of anointing with fragrant perfume is the customary treatment of honoured guests at the table and shows respect as well as refreshment (Luke 7:46).

Sheep were anointed with an oil that brought them peace and contentment. At certain times of the year flies caused great aggravation and problems to the sheep. The flies often landed upon the upper lip and laid their eggs. The larvae immediately went to the nearest dark area, the nose, and caused the sheep great torment and distraction. The role of the shepherd was to put oil over the head and face of the sheep to repel the flies, which brought soothing, peace and healing.

One of Satan's names is Beelzebub meaning 'Lord of the flies.' As we come under attack by the enemy, we can know the anointing of the Holy Spirit, strengthening us to deal with any torment of rejection. You can see here the role of the Holy Spirit as we respond to Him and receive by faith our daily anointing.

v5, *My cup overflows*
As we drink of the Spirit we can know refreshment, which will release an overflow in response to God of worship and praise. Overflow means abundance and our God is lavish in His giving to us to the point where we brim over with life (John 10:10). The pouring does not stop when the cup is filled. This is the favour and grace of God. Grace is favour we do not deserve, favour we cannot earn and favour we do not have to work for because it is freely given. Being "in Christ" means living in the overflow of his life. There are some people who say we have nothing to be thankful for. With this attitude rejection will make inroads into lives. God has given us so much, so why not step out and live in the joy of it.

v6, *surely goodness and mercy shall follow me*
The word surely means most definitely, absolutely and unconditionally.

There is no question and no doubt! The Good Shepherd was there for us at the beginning and will be at the end. His loving kindness is continual, consistent and constant. This will never be reversed! That is the sum of His commitment to us. All we can do is let Him take rejection in exchange for goodness and mercy. We leave our pain and hurt at the cross and remember goodness and mercy is always with us.

v6, *all the days of my life*
This speaks of our destiny. He is with us to lead and direct us into the best He has for us.

v6, *I will dwell in the house of the Lord forever*
He wants us to dwell, to settle down, to rest and to know His peace; that is His 'Shalom.' This is wholeness, spirit, soul and body. We dwell in His house meaning you and me with Him in us and us in him forever.

DAVID'S ANSWER TO THE PAIN IN HIS OWN LIFE

v3, *He restores my soul*
Restore means to bring back, to cause life to return, to revive or to invigorate. Sometimes we feel that life has drained away and we have nothing left. We feel like the sheep, that has wandered away or strayed and cannot find its way back. We can receive new life again because He says so and is committed to give it to us.

In this context the soul refers to our core, our heart or our spirit. When exhausted, weary or sad He causes life to return by restoring, re-animating and filling with new hope and joy. He cherishes, cares and values us as the shepherd does. It is a fantastic promise. All we can do is call on Him, making right choices in the process.

Remember the sheep on its back. It is known as a cast sheep, a sheep that has somehow rolled over onto its back with its legs up in air and looks dead.

The cast sheep cannot help itself. No matter how hard it tries it has to wait for the shepherd to come and help. The cast sheep may have been heavy with wool or lying on uneven ground when it lost its balance, rolled over and became helpless, unable to get up. It will not be long before it dies.

Cast in the personal context of a rejected person means downhearted, depressed, dispirited, demoralised, discouraged, pushed aside and discarded.

When a shepherd revives a cast down sheep, he reassures it, massages the heart, its legs and the length of its body to restore circulation. Then he gently turns the sheep over, lifts it up, and supports it so it can regain its equilibrium. The shepherd then puts the sheep on its feet, continuing to hold it and finally releases it, to return to the rest of the flock even though it may be a while. If it happens again the shepherd will repeat the process because he so values the life of the sheep he will not give up. The shepherd will carefully look over his flock day by day in case any are missing or cast down. What amazing grace and mercy we see in the shepherd. What amazing grace and mercy our Shepherd God has towards us.

What did David do when he felt cast down? He spoke to himself, *"Why are you cast down, O my soul, why are you disquieted within me"* (Psalm 42:11)? We sometimes need to have a word with ourselves! This can be a good thing as we focus on ourselves in a positive manner. A cast sheep is helpless as it becomes immobilised. People with rejection understand this. Even the healthiest sheep are vulnerable.

When David became totally isolated and rejected at Ziglag (see last chapter) when the Amalekites had abducted many families, he did one thing that became a turning point for him. He encouraged himself and found strength in the Lord his God (1 Samuel 30:6). David had nothing left and his men, in their own pain, talked about killing him. All he could do was hope in his God (Psalm 42:5-6). God is unchangeable therefore His grace is constant.

So as we reach out in our pain, His grace becomes sufficient. We may recognise we are cast down, but we do have the ability in Jesus to cast down imaginations, arguments and thoughts of the heart too (2 Corinthians 10:3-5). We can break down the walls in our own lives and take our thoughts captive and make them obedient to Christ.

We can also learn to cast our cares on Christ because He cares for us (1 Peter 5:7). If we feel or if we know we are cast down, we can cast down our negative thoughts and cast them upon Jesus! The word cast can be compared with flinging the fishing line far out into the river. So as we take responsibility for our own personal issues, we make a choice to let them go by casting them upon Him for Jesus is the only one who can take them away.

Memory Points

- Jesus is the Good Shepherd who is kind and caring.
- The Good Shepherd knows His sheep and they know Him.
- Psalm 23 and David's response to the Good Shepherd.
- The cast down sheep.
- Jesus restores our souls even when as sheep we are on our backs helpless.
- We can cast our cares upon Jesus because He cares for us.

THE REJECTED JESUS

Someone has said that Jesus was the most rejected person that ever lived. He identified with rejection in His life and death in a way that cannot be compared with anyone else. Most of us have to deal with rejection in our lives and as we consider Jesus, we will see the purpose of how and why He was rejected and how this has released hope, to enable us to live an overcoming life.

We have seen that rejection has been with us from the beginning of life, and how its source is spiritual, although it does affect us physically, mentally and emotionally. The pain of rejection can be traumatic and devastating, particularly as it affects every area of our lives.

We will consider how Jesus was affected by rejection from the beginning of His life in His mother's womb to His death on the cross. This will help us understand that because He overcame rejection, we can know freedom and healing in the power of His name. The amazing thing is that Jesus never let rejection overcome or control Him. He never manifested any fruit of rejection, because the roots were never allowed to take hold. Because Jesus identified with rejection so clearly, it means that He can identify with us in our pain.

He became as lowly as humanly and divinely possible, in order to lift us out of our rejection and into His acceptance and His Father's love. The divine exchange of the cross is 'our rejection for His acceptance' and it was only possible because He experienced the most horrendous rejection possible, which started before He was born.

His Birth And Early Years

The archangel Gabriel, one of God's most high ranking angels, came to Mary, a young teenager pledged to be married to a man called Joseph, and announced that God had chosen her to bear a child and that child was the Messiah (Luke 1:26-33). This created a colossal problem because under Jewish law, being pledged was as serious as being married. Joseph struggled so much that he decided to divorce her quietly. It was not his baby and the gossip, scandal and rumour would blaze around Nazareth. Everyone knew everyone and there must have been few secrets in that little town. It took another angel to convince Joseph and he married her (Matthew 1:19-21).

But who would believe this story? The baby is illegitimate and you cannot deny or disguise it! Joseph and Mary suffered the criticism, the humiliation and the shame alone.

At that time, a decree of Caesar created a tax, which meant Joseph should go to the city of his ancestors to be registered. It could not have been a worse time for Mary, as she was close to giving birth (Luke 2:1-5). There was a further problem, because they found there was no room anywhere for them to stay. Perhaps Joseph's family knew their stigma, so refused them. They were forced to find shelter in a cattle shed, which was the lower cave-like part of a house where the animals were kept. It was there that Jesus was born. After He was born, He was laid in a manger, which was an eating trough for the animals. He was wrapped in swaddling clothes probably old pieces of castoff clothing cut into strips (Luke 2:7).

Jesus was not born in Jerusalem in a palace but in Bethlehem, in a place where the animals were kept. He was not dressed in fine clothes but wrapped in rags. He was born in poverty. Jerusalem, the capital with the magnificent temple was a few miles to the north but Bethlehem was despised as the prophet indicated (Micah 5:2). There was nothing to boast about being born in Bethlehem. Jesus was born an outcast, rejected by humanity.

He was born during the reign of a wicked and ruthless king. Herod was disturbed when he heard that Magi from the east had arrived in Jerusalem, asking to see the King of the Jews, who had just been born. Herod found out that the Messiah was to be born in Bethlehem and sent the Magi there. The Magi were warned in a dream not to go back to Jerusalem and fled, while an Angel appeared to Joseph and told him to escape to Egypt, as Herod wanted to kill Jesus. When Herod heard this, in his fury he had all of the boys in Bethlehem less than two years old, murdered (Matthew 2:1-15). Interestingly enough, it was the chief priests and teachers of the law who told Herod about the Messiah being born in Bethlehem, which begs the question - why did they not go to worship him?

Indirectly Jesus' birth was the cause of many other deaths. Herod hated Jesus and wanted Him killed. The chief priests and the other leaders had no time for Jesus and this rejection by them continued throughout His entire ministry until they killed Him. His birth and early years had much stigma attached to it and, as we summarise His early beginnings, it is not difficult to see the strong thread of rejection throughout His life. Jesus suffered rejection from the very beginning of His life.

AT HOME

Jesus lived in a nation that was severely oppressed by another nation and, being a Jew, He knew His race was despised by other surrounding nations. Jesus was a rejected person, living in a rejected nation, which was under the iron rule of the Romans. He would also have been racially abused. When Nathaniel was told about Jesus he stated, *"can anything good come out of Nazareth"* (John 1:46). In Jesus' time there was great prejudice against Nazareth. It was seen as contemptible and even despised by its neighbours, the Galileans. It was known as such a miserable place that no one could ever think of something good coming out of it. It was a nondescript town miles from anywhere, except for the lavish and luxurious city built by King Herod.

At one time in His ministry, Jesus' relatives and friends could not handle the fact that so many people wanted to hear Him. They decided to take charge of Him themselves, and took Him home as they thought He was out of His mind, delirious or deranged because He was proclaiming He was the Messiah. What sensible person would throw away his job to become a wandering preacher - even His own brothers would not believe Him (Mark 3:21, John 7:5). It is so sad when your own family take this stance with you. Jesus' family misunderstood Him and therefore basically rejected Him.

His Own People

Rejection started in Jesus' hometown when He visited the synagogue. The people who had known Him all His life did not like what He was saying. They listened to Him at first but turned on Him in anger and tried to kill Him as they drove Him out of town where they tried to throw Him over a cliff (Luke 4:28-30). Later, they took offence again and were very cynical asking where a carpenter gets wisdom and miraculous powers. They asked who He thought He was, because they thought He was inferior. They called Him a Samaritan, which was a great insult to a Jew in those days and they told Him He was demonised (John 10:20). They did not like Him going to the house of Zacchaeus, a 'sinner'. Zacchaeus was happy though because Jesus met him in his rejection and accepted him (Luke 19:7). At the end the Jews demanded the death of Jesus and continually mocked and insulted Him as He hung on the cross (Matthew 27:39-44).

This can all be summed up in the scripture, *'He was in the world, and though the world was made through Him, the world did not recognise Him. He came to that which was His own, but His own did not receive Him'* (John 1:10-11 NIV). His own people rejected Him.

HIS MINISTRY, HIS DISCIPLES, HIS FRIENDS

The message of Jesus was hard to accept even by His disciples. They often grumbled and when Jesus confronted them many turned back and no longer followed Him. He even asked the twelve if they wanted to leave Him too. He could have been left on His own. When Jesus said to the disciples that they would all fall away they could not believe it and denied it, but we know what happened (John 6:60-68).

- Jesus was not welcome in a Samaritan village (Luke 9:53).
- Even Peter, who seemed to take the lead in declaring he would never leave saying, "I am ready to go with you to prison and death, I will never disown you," denied him at the end (Luke 22:33).
- He was betrayed by one of the disciples, Judas (Luke 22:3-7, 47-48).
- At His greatest trial, before the cross in the garden of Gethsemane, His friends fell asleep. He came to them three times in anguish and found them heavy with sleep each time (Mark 14:37-41).
- Everyone deserted Him and fled even a young man who was with Him and was seized by the guards tore himself away and fled naked (Mark 14:50-52).

Throughout the three years of his ministry, Jesus experienced constant rejection. He even talked about it himself in order to prepare the disciples for the crucifixion (Luke 9:22).

Jesus kept surprising everybody especially those who followed Him. He would do things differently like eat at the wrong house, talk to the wrong people, talk to trees or the weather and heal on the wrong day. Where Jesus was there was unpredictability and He made people uncomfortable. It was as though there was something dangerous, uncontrollable, threatening, outside the norm and the status quo. Jesus did not care about who He was close to, who He spoke to, who He ate with, who He let touch Him and therefore broke some of the laws, which discriminated against so many people. Jesus was radical especially with the social and cultural rules. He took grace beyond the limits. It was this that got Him into so much trouble. The amazing thing is that even after three years with Jesus continuously, very few of His friends were with Him at the end.

HIS OWN WORDS

Jesus repeatedly talked about His coming rejection and death.

- *"The Son of Man must suffer many things and be rejected by the elders, chief priests and the lawyers"* (Luke 9:22).
- *"The Son of Man is going to be betrayed into the hands of men"* (Luke 9:44).
- *"But first He must suffer many things and be rejected by this generation"* (Luke 17:25).
- *"The Son of Man will be handed over to the Gentiles. They will mock Him, insult Him, flog Him, spit on Him and kill Him"* (Matthew 20:17-19, Luke 18:32).

Yet His friends were so slow to understand Him. After the resurrection they remembered His words (Luke 24:8). Jesus knew what was going to happen to Him and how it was going to come to pass. Some of us find it difficult talking about the good things that happen to us, so it is almost inconceivable that He would talk in the way He did about His death.

THE WORDS OF THE PROPHETS

Hundreds of years before the birth of Jesus, the Old Testament prophets spoke about the type of man Jesus was and the sort of death He would go through. There are many prophecies regarding Jesus and some are specifically related to His rejection particularly in Isaiah 53.

"For He shall grow up before Him as a tender plant and as a root out of dry ground. He has no form or comeliness; and when we see Him, there is no beauty that we should desire Him" (Isaiah 53:2).

There was nothing about His physical appearance that made Jesus different from an ordinary Jewish man. There was nothing that caused people to take interest in Him. It seems He was not physically imposing. Jesus was rejected because He did not fit into Jewish preconceptions of what a Messiah was like.

"He was despised and rejected by men; a man of sorrows, and acquainted with grief. And as one from whom men hide their faces He was despised, and we esteemed Him not" (Isaiah 53:3).

The word despised means to be thought little of or worthless. He was not valued in any way at all.

- Jesus was despised enough to be betrayed by His own familiar friend.
- He was despised enough to be given a fake trial instead of a fair trial.
- He was despised enough to be mocked, spat upon, and beaten.
- He was despised enough to be forced into carrying His own cross, as far as He was able to carry it.
- The very people He came to save, especially their leadership despised Jesus.

This rejection brought sorrow and grief with intense emotional pain. Jesus was indeed a man of sorrows, very much acquainted with suffering. People rejected Him because they wanted a warrior not a carpenter; they wanted a king and not a servant, and He did not represent the important things that people wanted such as wealth.

In His rejection He was pierced and crushed, oppressed and afflicted and He took the abuse quietly. When being falsely accused, He said nothing. He was given a grave with the wicked when He had done nothing wrong. He was dishonoured in life and dishonoured in death. It seems inconceivable that Jesus our Messiah and Saviour, would not only be aware of these prophecies, but also understand them particularly when they continually spoke of His rejection.

THE LEADERS OF THE PEOPLE

- They claimed He was a blasphemer because He talked about forgiving sins (Mark 2:6-7).
- They criticised Him when He ate with 'sinners' and 'tax collectors' (Mark 2:16).
- When He healed on the Sabbath, they plotted to kill Him (Mark 3:6).
- They announced that Jesus was demonised (Mark 3:22).
- The leaders condemned Him because some of His disciples ate with unwashed hands (Mark 7:2-5).
- They were continually pushing Jesus to prove His miraculous power (Mark 8:11).
- The leaders tried to catch Him out with very awkward questions (Mark 10:2).
- Jesus' authority was continually questioned by them and not in the best spirit (Mark 11:28).
- The chief priests and the whole Sanhedrin finally tried to get evidence against Jesus to condemn Him. They could not so they falsely accused Him (Mark 14:55-59).

- The leaders insulted and mocked Him as He hung on the cross (Mark 15:31).

It is amazing how the religious and political leaders rejected Him. From the very beginning there was trouble because everyone saw that Jesus had authority and power (Luke 4:36) and that was rare in those days. Jesus began to attract the common people who followed Him gladly. The leaders saw their control challenged, as He began to undermine the traditions of Jewish society, such as the Sabbath. So they plotted to kill Him.

HIS GREATEST REJECTION

What can be more horrific and gruesome than being crucified. Accounts have been written describing the utterly intense physical and mental pain and agony Jesus suffered. Gethsemane was a prelude to the cross. It was there that Jesus agonised about what was to come, while His friends were asleep. It is hard to conceive the loneliness, isolation and desolation. He became so troubled and distressed that the stress within Him manifested physically and He sweat drops of blood. The strain broke the capillaries in His forehead and He began to bleed.

Then two amazing things happened, which seemed to be conflicting:

'He went a little farther, and fell on the ground, and prayed that if it were possible, the hour might pass from Him. Then he said, "Abba, Father, all things are possible for You. Take this cup away from Me; nevertheless, not what I will, but what You will"' (Mark 14:35-36). The pressure was so great on Him that He asked for another way. However, what He wanted to do most of all was the will of His Father, which was to die. Jesus uses a word for His Father that no Jew would ever use. He called Him "Abba". Some would translate this word as daddy. The deep intimacy of the relationship between the Son and His Father was expressed in this word, which gave Him the confidence to face what lay ahead.

Incredibly something else happened which is clearly set out in the prophets as well as the narrative in the Gospels. God actively punished Jesus to the point where Jesus could no longer even feel the presence of God, His Father.

'Now when the sixth hour had come, there was darkness over the whole land until the ninth hour. And at the ninth hour Jesus cried out with a loud voice, saying, "Eloi, Eloi, lama sabachthani?" which is translated, "my God, my God, why have you forsaken me"' (Mark 15:33-34).

Can we even imagine that this was in the plan of God? The relationship the Father and the Son had was so powerful, but both had to let it go, which led to the final rejection at the cross, when Jesus cried those awful piercing words. It was an indescribably loud cry with incredible anguish in the darkness. Forsaken means to separate, to abandon, to give up or to desert and Jesus was cut off from His Father.

Isaiah sums it up. *"Yet we considered Him stricken by God, smitten by Him and afflicted"* (Isaiah 53:4). *"It was the Lord's will to crush Him and cause Him to suffer"* (Isaiah 53:10 NIV).

It seemed as though God drew a veil across the sun, and in the darkness of those three hours, Jesus was made an offering for sin. God rejected Him in order to open the door of acceptance for us. It was the will of God, and that was the greatest rejection of all, yet it was not an evil deed but redemptive in the plan and purpose of God.

So, the rejection of Jesus was made complete at the cross when the Father turned His back on His Son. It was Their love for you and me that made it happen. The cross then provides a 'divine exchange' for us. Instead of being and feeling rejected, we can receive healing, acceptance, affirmation, love, security and so much more through the death and resurrection of Jesus.

FINALLY

The one, who experienced the ultimate rejection, death on a cross, will welcome anyone. Jesus said, *"However, those the Father has given Me will come to Me, I will never reject them"* (John 6:37 NLT).

Our Heavenly Father says the same, *"never will I leave you; never will I forsake you"* (Hebrews 13:5-6, Deuteronomy 31:6). So if the Lord is with us what can we fear?

The Father forsook the Son in order to keep His promise to us. He will never reject us.

MEMORY POINTS

- Rejection affected Jesus right through His life.
- He identified with rejection from the beginning to the end of His life.
- All areas of society including His family rejected Jesus.
- He never let rejection overcome Him or control Him.
- The words of the Prophets predicted His rejection.
- The greatest rejection was that of His Father when the Father turned His back on His Son at the cross.
- The purpose of Jesus' coming was to draw us to the love of the Father and in the divine exchange of the cross that was fulfilled. His rejection became our acceptance.

IN THE BEGINNING

Going back to the beginning or the source of something is often the key to understanding its nature, which will lead to knowledge of what to do and how to deal with it. The origin of rejection starts at the beginning of humanity, as we know it, and clearly shows that rejection has been around as long as man and woman have. It is an integral part of life for a large percentage of society. Therefore, looking at how rejection affected our first parents and its consequences for them and their children, will give us an understanding and awareness of how rejection began and how it affects us now.

WITH GOD IN A GARDEN

God put a man in a garden to work it and to take care of it. He had formed and fashioned man from the dust of the earth and, amazingly, breathed His breath into him to give him life, God's life (Genesis 2:7). There is a Jewish belief that 'God is in search of humanity for love and relationship; that God is in pursuit of us.' Because of the glorious fellowship of the Trinity - Father, Son and Holy Spirit - God was not alone. However, when God created the earth with man and woman in it, His desire was to have a relationship with them. This has to be the ultimate in acceptance and love and it is underlined because God had purposed to come down to where we are, rather than to have us struggle to find or reach Him. This was made clear when Jesus came to earth, as the Word was made flesh to make His dwelling amongst us (John 1:14 NIV).

God's plan for relationship was not complete because man was alone. God said, *"it is not good for man to be alone; I will make him a helper, suitable for him"* (Genesis 2:18, 21-24). We read that God took a rib from the man and created woman to be with him and compliment him. It was a three-fold cord, the man, woman and God, intertwined for commitment and strength in relationship.

The garden became a place of harmony, of complete relationship, where a man and a woman commune and communicate with each other and their God. They were fulfilled in their manhood and womanhood, in their masculinity and femininity, in their sexuality. They were totally affirmed and accepted in their identity, and secure in their role, which brought a unity in all they did. They reflected the Glory of the Father completely. There was a true sense of worth and belonging as they lived in the garden and met with God. It is summed up so beautifully, *"God saw all that He made and it was very good"* (Genesis 1:31). Not good, but very good. When God says good that is amazing but when He says very good that is awesome.

It was here in the garden that God gave the man and woman a commission that was to last for ever. God blessed them and said to them, *"be fruitful and increase in number; fill the earth and subdue it and rule over every living creature"* (Genesis 1:28). This can be defined as be fruitful, which is sexual, subdue, which is authority and rule, which is spiritual. God gave them everything they required to live on this earth with satisfaction and fulfilment. Notice it was together, they were co-regents, ruling together in a mutual submission. This meant equality with each other, which brought glorious blessing as they communed with their God.

Often Adam and Eve heard the sound of God walking in the garden and they were at one with Him. It is difficult to imagine such a manifestation of life, sound and glory when God came down to walk with them. The garden demonstrates heaven on earth being a place of peace, and fulfilment for the purpose of God was to reach them and not to demand they try to reach Him. God is passionate about coming down to where we are, to commune and to communicate. God was with them as He is with us, loving and accepting us.

RESPONSIBILITY

It was in this idyllic place that God gave a command to the man, *"You are free to eat of every tree in the garden but you must not eat from the tree of the knowledge of good and evil, for when you eat of it you will surely die"* (Genesis 2:16-17).

What is most important to remember is that God had given man a free will, with the right to choose and to take responsibility. True fulfilment only comes with the ability and freedom to make right choices. Adam had another responsibility because all of this happened before the woman was created, and he needed to tell her about God's command. Whether he did or not we do not know but the consequences were disastrous.

THE ENEMY

It was into the garden that Satan came to undermine the relationship the man and the woman had with God and each other. Satan was the angel who tried to take God's throne from Him but he was banished from heaven to earth and humanity became the target. Satan was after the authority that God had given man and woman. They had something he wanted and he was out to take it, so he struck at the heart of the issue when he undermined Adam and Eve's relationship with their God and each other.

He first challenged the woman by bringing doubt to God's word. Then he tempted her with a desire for much more and, finally, blatantly told her that God's words about dying were not true. Interestingly and cleverly, he came to the woman first because God had spoken to Adam about this and not her. She responded by telling Satan what God had said. The fruit of the tree was good, pleasing and desirable and, as she ate, she gave some to the man - but remember God clearly said, *"do not eat of it."*

The question is where was the man when she ate the fruit. Right by the side of the woman, meaning he must have heard the conversation with Satan. He actually said nothing and did nothing. He had his own accountability in this.

God gave them a command but also a free will, a right to choose, which meant they both had responsibility. They decided in their greed to reach out for more - to be like God. There was nothing more, of course, except deception and ultimately emptiness and rejection. God has given us all a right to make decisions. This is responsibility. We have the ability to make right or wrong choices. Adam and Eve made a wrong choice and we have all suffered for it. They not only disobeyed God but also rebelled against him and, therefore, rejected him. As a consequence their eyes were opened, they realised what they had done and instead of innocence, there was shame. The enemy undermined God's word, gave them false expectations and distorted their image of themselves as children of God. He damaged their relationship with God and with each other.

Actually, when their eyes were open, they saw something they did not expect. It was not the glory of being like God, but they saw their literal nakedness. They were also naked inside; having been stripped of all God gave them. Fear and shame confronted them and consequently rejection. They attempted to cover themselves, then run and hide. The enemy said they would have more, but they ended up with nothing.

THE CURSE

Usually when God came into the garden, there was joy and great fellowship, for it was a time when God was with His creation (Genesis 3:8). The word walking also means strolling. Does that mean God strolled through the garden in a leisurely, unhurried, slow and gentle way? Yes, for God had time for Adam and Eve. This is closeness and intimacy. This is soaking in the presence of God. *"I will walk among you and be your God and you shall be my people"* (Leviticus 26:12). However, this time when God came, Adam and Eve were hidden, they were afraid, they had rejected God's ways. When they realised they were naked, they tried in a pathetic manner to cover themselves and hide from God. *'God called to the man, "Where are you"'* (Genesis 3:9 NIV)? As if God did not know where they were! God is still asking us today, "Where are you?"

Adam and Eve had lost their identity but neither of them would take responsibility. The man blamed the woman and God; he took no responsibility. The woman blamed the devil and she did take some responsibility (Genesis 3:11-13). We do tend to shift blame and accuse easily. It is always someone else's fault.

God made them all accountable. They had lost their spiritual, mental, emotional and physical harmony with each other and God. Because they rejected Him, He had no choice but to banish them from the garden just as He had banished Satan from heaven. If they had eaten from the tree of life after taking fruit from the tree of knowledge of good and evil as they used to, all would have been lost. They would have lived forever in their sin. They lost their pure sexuality, their spirituality, their authority, their inheritance and death had set in. Their role and identity had changed forever. They must have been overwhelmed with emotions they had never felt as they left the garden. They lost their inheritance, their sonship and relationship with the Father. Rejection had taken root. Homeless, fatherless and without identity Adam and Eve became orphans and the first to know rejection.

Regretfully the consequences were soon to affect their first two sons.

God was clear in His judgement (Genesis 3:16). He said there would be, *"pain in childbirth."* Conception, pregnancy and childbirth would never be the same. *"Your desire shall be for your husband."* The woman turned from God and her own relationship with Him and turned towards her husband, which meant that she was under his control. *"He shall rule over you."* This is female subordination and was never God's way. This has become so contentious in the church and outside of it. Her equality with her husband changed, and inferiority to him was established and it became 'man is head and man rules.' Being banished and rejected from God's presence caused this, but we can go back to God's original purposes living in harmony with Him and in love and acceptance with each other. Adam and Eve left the garden with serious consequences to their sin. Their relationship had changed forever. Eve was no longer equal but in subjection, under Adam's authority. Rejection had also taken root in humanity.

WHAT DID GOD DO?

His righteous judgement meant banishing them from the garden but His grace and mercy is evident. The Lord Himself made garments of skin for Adam and Eve and covered them (Genesis 3:21). He killed an animal, and while the blood was still warm made coats for them so that their nakedness was not revealed. Sacrifice, with the shedding of blood became the only way humanity was able to meet with God. This can be seen throughout the Old Testament. It was the plan for redemption, culminating finally with the blood of Jesus being shed at the cross for you and me. Even in the midst of the pain, the shame and rejection with awful separation, God wanted to bring humanity back to Himself through the shedding of blood. This was the first time that blood was shed and it was the only way to bring humanity back to Him. That is redemption.

MEMORY POINTS

- We need to be aware of the significance of these early passages in Genesis and their link to rejection, for the source and roots of rejection are there.
- It is clear that rejection has been around as long as man and woman have been living. The lives of the first family are such a key to rejection. We need to take note.
- The disobedience in the garden has affected the way men and women behave with each other. It is birthed in control, for both want the power and they will dominate, intimidate and manipulate to get it. Rejection is behind this.
- Rejection can be hereditary. There is a curse that will come from the third and fourth generations (Exodus 34:6-7).
- Satan and his demonic powers have a great part to play in rejection.
- Our power to choose and our free will is important in rejection. We have a personal responsibility and we need to understand this.
- What we see are the consequences of making a wrong choice and the reaction that went with it. The man blamed God and the woman; then the woman blamed the enemy. No one took personal responsibility for his or her own actions.
- This chapter leads us to the significance and ultimately the consequence of rejection in the garden, yet the hope we have is in what happened in another garden thousands of years later when Jesus died.

THE GARDEN

The consequence of Adam and Eves' sin not only affected them and their children, but it still affects us.

Adam and Eve were isolated, lonely and damaged. Their rejection of God and of His word had changed everything. They felt, and were, a rejected couple. Even the animals and the land seemed against them. It was in this situation they had children. Cain, the oldest, and his brother Abel were very different.

It seems that much of the rejection the parents had been affected by passed to Cain. He was clearly affected by the sin of his parents and his sense of choice, reason, and behaviour showed it. Adam and Eve had given Satan a right that did not finish with them. The whole of the human race has been affected. Yet even in Cain's sin and disobedience, we will see that God graciously gave him another chance.

CAIN, ABEL AND GOD

The boys were so different in many ways, even in the way they worked. Abel became a shepherd and Cain a farmer, and they brought different offerings from their produce to God. Their parents must have told them about their beginnings; those final days as they left the garden and God's response of grace, the garments of skin to cover them. They would have been taught how to respond to God with offerings, yet their offerings were so different and only one of the offerings was accepted. Cain brought some of the fruits of the soil and Abel brought the fat portions of the first fruits of his flock. God looked with favour on Abel but not Cain (Genesis 4:2-5 NIV).

Why did this happen? Obviously the offerings came later as the boys were coming into manhood and it would appear they knew what was acceptable to God, but Cain took no notice.

What did the offerings mean? Simply they meant an expression of gratitude to God for all that they had been given and a request for favour and blessing. The great faith chapter of the New Testament tells us, *"Abel offered a better sacrifice"* (Hebrews 11:4 NIV).

It was the type of sacrifice and the attitude of heart that was better. Abel had faith in God and expressed that by shedding the blood of a lamb. Cain wanted God to accept the works of his own hands and to affirm him for what he had done. You can never please God in that way. Nothing we do in trying to please God by works or performance will be accepted. We offer by faith as Abel did. He had a depth of faith that his brother did not have. He understood that the sacrifice of a life was the only offering acceptable to God. Cain offered something lifeless indicating his arrogance, independence and pride. Abel's faith is underlined further, as scripture compares him with Jesus' offering. Just as Abel's offering was better than Cain's, so the sacrifice of Jesus spoke of better things (Hebrews 12:24). It became a proclamation of grace.

Because of this Cain was not just angry but very angry. His face was downcast and he looked dejected and sad. This could be seen as a mixture of depression, self-pity and rebellion. God had looked with favour on Abel's offering but He did not receive Cain's at all. What an incredible reaction Cain had. He was angry with God and his brother. He seemed to blame everyone except himself. It has been said that blame is merely a way to discharge pain and discomfort, and maybe his discomfort just showed his irresponsibility in this.

Cain was rejected because he sought God on his own terms, which was what caused the fall of his parents in the first place. Cain wanted to control the situation. Control means power over something or someone. He thought he had the right to decide what should be acceptable to God.

God's response to Cain is amazing. He gives Cain another chance. He asks Cain a question, which of course He knows the answer to, but does require an honest response. This is grace, kindness and consideration but there is also advice and a warning. God begins to reason with Cain and gives him an opportunity to get it right, *"If you do what is right, will you not be accepted"* Genesis 4:6-7). Yet Cain wanted it right his way, not God's way. Rebellion replaces God's will with our own. Cain wanted to do it his way. Surely he would have known there was a right way. God was looking for a heart response in obedience to Him but all He received was rejection from Cain.

THE WARNING

God showed Cain what was happening in the invisible spiritual realm. *"If you do not do what is right, sin is crouching at the door; it desires to have you, but you must master it"* (Genesis 4:7 NIV). The word sin could be interpreted as a demon waiting at the door for an opportunity. It was clearly Cain's responsibility to make the right choice. It seemed that Cain wanted to blame everyone else, rather than take any responsibility himself. The word master means to overcome. If God says we can overcome, by His grace and in His name, we can.

THE CONSEQUENCES

Sadly, Cain rejected God and His grace. The fermenting anger and hatred had to be released somewhere else. Innocently Abel went with his brother for a walk, and shockingly, Cain murdered him (Genesis 4:8). Incredibly, God heard the cry of the blood of Abel. How could that happen? Blood is life and when blood is shed life is poured out. Abel's lifeblood cried out to God (Genesis 4:10). God questioned Cain who responded in an aggressive and defiant manner. In his rebellion he answered, *"am I my brother's keeper."* As well as being hard-hearted, insensitive and indifferent, he was again rejecting God.

Just as Cain's parents were sent away, so was Cain. The result was a curse. Cain had every opportunity to change and be accepted. He had rejected God and His ways and became the victim of his own choices. God decreed that Cain should be a restless wanderer throughout the earth (Genesis 4:12).

The expression restless wanderer is very significant in rejection. Rejection is linked to identity and image. The restless wanderer never finds fulfilment in what he or she is. There is no satisfaction in his role as a person. Something is always driving him to something more. Unfortunately like Adam and Eve and now Cain something more is never there. This restlessness is a control that drives a person so that they are never satisfied in who they are and what they do. This is the source of rejection. The heart of God is rest. Time and time again throughout the scriptures God is looking for a place of rest with His people. He said, *"My Presence will go with you, and I will give you rest"* (Exodus 33:14). Rejection is the exact opposite. It controls you by driving you to find that rest by your own actions, your own performance. However our relationship with God starts in rest. We do not have to find it. We are in it. Satan and his demonic powers seem to thrive on restlessness as it gives them an opportunity to harass.

Cain's response to God in the context of rejection is important to look at (Genesis 4:13-16). He said to God:

- *"My punishment is more than I can bear,"* which communicates self-pity, despair, hopelessness and probably self-rejection.
- *"You are driving me from the land,"* which suggests Cain is accusing and then blaming God for his own irresponsibility. He would probably still have been very angry with God.
- *"I will be hidden from your presence."* Cain has previously shown no desire to be in God's presence, so was this an irrational attempt to pressurise God to change His mind?
- *"Whoever finds me will kill me,"* which is fear, including fear of rejection and fear of death. However, God in His grace and mercy protected Cain by marking him, so that anyone who recognised him would not kill him. There is no evidence to show what the mark was. God gave it to Cain to distinguish him from the rest of mankind.

Right at the end of the New Testament Cain is mentioned in two passages. It is more than intriguing that this happened. What Cain and his parents did affected the whole of humanity. There are keys here to overcoming rejection.

"Do not be like Cain" (1 John 3:11-12), but love one another just as Jesus did. This is the antithesis of rejection. Love of God, of self and one another will dissolve rejection.

"The way of Cain" (Jude 11) is the way of rebellion and disobedience motivated by restlessness and pride and self-interest.

THE BRIDE, THE GROOM AND THE HEAVENLY FATHER

This is another perspective to consider; a key to the revelation of the

Father's love, not just for Adam and Eve, but for us too as it shows how to begin to understand and learn to deal with rejection.

As Eve ate the fruit Adam had a major decision to make. Admittedly it had to be quick and the question is, how prepared was he to make the right choice? Did he realise the consequences? Adam was in a massive dilemma. What should he do? How could he choose between the Father and the bride? Adam was the Father's son and he had a wonderful bride. He loved his Heavenly Father and he loved his bride. He realised he would have to give up one of them for the sake of the other.

Should he reject her in his love for and obedience to God, or in his love for her, stand in rebellion against God and eat the fruit with her, which would mean separation from God. Would the man want to live eternally separated from his bride when he loved her? He must have been so torn between his love for the bride and his relationship with the Father. If Adam chose Eve, what would that do to his relationship with the Father? It would mean that choosing his bride over God would separate them from God.

Adam left his relationship with the Father to go to his bride. He rejected the Father for the bride, which meant separation and severance. Adam deliberately turned away from God and all His promises and his inheritance in preference for the love of his heart. His choice started something that would never end, unless someone could redeem the situation.

Through Adam's choice, sin entered the world but it was not only that, for I believe this was the beginning of rejection not only for Adam and Eve but also for humanity. If you leave the Father's love you are on your own. The relationship with God the Father is severed, so there is no communication or expression of love, and the heart has not got the security it needs.

Adam and Eve made the wrong choice and humanity has suffered the consequences ever since. They disobeyed God, rebelled against Him and chose to reject Him and His ways. Their first-born son, Cain, did the same thing and ultimately became a restless wanderer, which is the nature of rejection. The grace of God was so apparent to Cain, even when he had reacted in anger at God. He refused his Heavenly Father's plea to take responsibility and make a right choice. Humanity has been left with an inheritance, which has become so destructive.

WHAT HAPPENED WHEN JESUS DIED

In the place where Jesus died there was a garden (John 19:41) and in that garden there was a tomb, where Jesus was buried. It was known as the garden tomb. There was a garden in the beginning with the first Adam and a garden at the cross for the last Adam, Jesus. What ended in Eden started again in the garden in Jerusalem.

At the cross when the Father rejected the Son, and there was a divine exchange of acceptance in place of rejection, reconciliation took place as the blood of Jesus was shed. This was the culmination of the time in Eden when God covered Adam and Eve with the bloodied skin of the animal and when the blood of God bought back an unredeemed humanity (Acts 20:28).

Therefore we can come back into a very personal relationship with God through Jesus knowing that we are accepted. We are not lost and those words, "where are you?" need not apply any more. We know where we are and we know who we are. We have access to the presence of God.

MEMORY POINTS

- Rejection did not stay with Adam and Eve. It passed into the next generation and hence affected all of humanity.
- Cain and Abel were so different as were their offerings to God. God accepted Abel's, but not Cain's.

- Abel pleased God through the sacrifice of a lamb and the shedding of blood, but Cain tried to please God with the works of his own hands.
- Abel moved by faith but Cain was arrogant, independent and proud.
- Cain's attitude was reactionary and angry with God and even though God gave him a second chance Cain rejected him and then murdered his brother. His attitude of heart was truly exposed.
- The consequences were severe with Cain refusing to take responsibility and he was banished to become a restless wanderer.
- The term restless wanderer is a key in defining rejection.
- St Augustine said to God, "we were made for You and our hearts are restless until they rest in You."

ROOTS & FRUIT

Many years ago when I was working as a Chartered Surveyor valuing residential property for mortgage, tree roots could become a problem to houses in certain conditions either climate, different types of soil or if the tree was too close to the property. If a tree is closer than its height from a building it is possible, due to the roots growing under the property, for structural movement and instability to take place. Roots are attracted to water and will be drawn to it however close to a property. They will take sustenance out of the soil and in dry seasons, the soil will contract. In all probability, in view of the weight of the property, foundations will move and subsidence will take place. The remedy is not only dealing with the roots of the tree but also the time consuming and costly business of underpinning the foundations and repairing any cracks. Roots therefore, can do a lot of damage to a property.

The roots of a plant or tree anchors and establishes it into the ground, holding it in position, absorbing water and other nutrients to sustain it and give it life. Roots are the hidden parts under the ground that often become long and deep and, if they need removing, can be exceedingly difficult.

In the context of rejection, roots are crucial as they follow the same principle. They cannot be ignored and are often deep and long, having developed over many years and will need careful and sensitive handling when they become exposed.

As seeds of rejection are planted, when the conditions are right, it is not long before roots begin to grow. If the roots are nurtured over the years, a tree of rejection will begin to appear producing all kinds of fruit, which manifest through the character and personality of a person. This can become time consuming in counselling and ministry as it is often the foundation or core of a life that has been exposed to rejection.

It is relatively easy to pick fruit from a tree, but much more difficult to deal with the roots and if they are not exposed and dug up, the fruit will grow again and again. *"I destroyed his fruit above and his roots below"* (Amos 2:9). It is essential therefore, to consider and identify the roots before dealing with the fruit.

CONTROL

Before considering the three areas that sum up the roots of rejection, it is most important to look at the issue of control in this context. Control is very much connected to rejection, and as well as defining it, we will see how much it affects each of the three roots of rejection.

In the context of rejection, control has to do with power over people by making them do what we want through domination, manipulation and intimidation. It is taking away a person's right to make decisions and take responsibility for themselves. It is subtle and often goes unnoticed until it is too late. That is why spiritually it is a principle compared or connected to witchcraft, as it is a power issue. The root of rebellion (see below) highlights this.

Many rejected people have lived under this type of control, and will consistently use it to feed their own sense of rejection. It becomes a safe survival technique. Perceived conditional acceptance such as, "It's very nice but..." leads to an inability to trust. Rejection creates an overriding, desperate need to be in control of your own life and other people, which can lead to feeling possessive and jealous on the one hand, or threatened and angry on the other. The mix of rejection and control is powerful and dangerous.

- Domination is an authoritarian expression of trying to run or rule someone else's life.
- Manipulation is a way of trying to change someone through emotional pressure, or deception. In the context of rejection it is all about doing what you can to gain acceptance. You do not care what you do, you just cannot be alone living with your rejection, so making someone dependant on you through guilt, or some other emotional method is your answer.
- Intimidation is intentional behaviour where by making a person fearful you actually control to get your own way. Rejected people in their anger can overawe others because of their force of personality.

Controlling relationships like this can create an unhealthy attachment, dependency and co-dependency.

THE ROOT OF REBELLION

Rebellion is an aggressive reaction, which shows itself in resistance to, or in total disregard of the person who is perceived or alleged to show rejection. When the rejected person reacts in this manner, anyone who gets in his or her way can be affected. You feel they are against you. The emotional reaction can be expressed through a display of anger, arrogance or criticism, which can remain deeply hidden. At some stage however, there will probably be an eruption and anyone too close will be damaged. Many people with this root just hurt themselves through self-hate, self-criticism or self-harm. It can also be expressed in defiance or antagonism.

Rebellion in a biblical sense is in the same category as witchcraft (1 Samuel 15:23). This is not meant to give fear but just to bring a definition into context. The rebellious live in a dry land (Psalm 68:6), which denotes spiritual dehydration so that relationship with God will be undermined. This practice can ultimately open a door to the demonic.

Rebellion And Control

When someone feels threatened or out of control they will possibly react by vowing, "no one is going to control me; no one is going to make decisions for me." The attitude of always being right becomes hard to penetrate. In this capacity the Holy Spirit can be grieved (Ephesians 4:30-31). The Holy Spirit is a divine personality and may withdraw if our actions and reactions are sinful. He does not control but we can and the demonic will, if given the right.

Some people think they can control if they hurt other people or if they hurt themselves. "I'll control my own circumstances and I'll make sure I control and intimidate the people around me."

Often those born in rejection are predisposed to be angry. Anger or other strong emotions can intimidate and control even from an early age. Someone like this can become hostile to anyone who stands in their way. They tend to disrespect others verbally or give them the silent treatment. Fear of being alone and rejected can also cause a person to seek attention in a wrong way.

THE ROOT OF SELF-REJECTION

Self-rejection is what it says it is. Rejection is turned inwards, becoming a strong and powerful root, which will not stop growing while it is being fed by thoughts, words and actions of self-rejection. When we reject ourselves, we will finally reject the God who made us. Self-rejection can also lead to self-harm and suicidal thoughts. Using words, which create negative self-belief, will cause damage emotionally and mentally.

Self-Rejection And Control

The power of the mind and the tongue can bring such destruction. Life and death is in the power of the tongue and we need to choose which one to live by (Proverbs 18:21). You can manage your own life. You have the ability to make decisions whether they are right or wrong. You have the power to accept or reject yourself and you have the power to choose life or death. You can get to the place where you decide you do not like yourself. There must be something wrong with you, for people do not seem to like you and are uncomfortable with you. To be safe, you tell yourself you have the power to do or say what you like, and nobody can stop you.

The term 'curse' may seem an antiquated word. It means to speak, declare or pronounce evil, abuse or misfortune over someone, something or yourself. It could mean appealing to a supernatural power to come and do harm.

Another term linked to curse in this context is the 'inner vow.' An inner vow is a promise made by you to you. For example you have been hurt once again and you get to the place in your pain and anger where you clearly and strongly speak into yourself with a vow. You are determined not to allow yourself to be hurt and rejected again so you use the word, 'I'll never...' Using the words 'I will' makes a powerful statement. Its strength can affect us body, soul and spirit.

The deception comes when you think these vows make you safe. They are false and dangerous and create barriers that you think will protect you but they lock you in and it becomes more difficult to listen to God and other caring people. Putting a judgement on yourself is self-rejection. In building barriers you touch the root of self-protection or fear of rejection, and if the reaction is anger or despair you connect with the root of rebellion.

Bear in mind that curses and inner vows go deep and certainly if spoken in childhood can be forgotten, which does not mean they disappear. They are triggered by circumstance or situation. Thoughts such as, "I wish I was..." can be effective especially when we are angry with ourselves. Words are so powerful we can become what we say we are.

There are many examples of the curse and inner vow:

- "I will never be worth anything."
- "I will never trust again."
- "I will never show emotion."
- "I will never make it because I am no good."
- "I hate myself, I am too tall, too short, too fat, too thin or I am ugly."
- "I am useless, I am a failure or I will never achieve."
- "I will never change."

"As soon as someone accuses me or criticizes me, as soon as I am rejected, left alone, or abandoned, I find myself thinking that it proves once again that I am nobody, I am no good, I deserve to be pushed aside, forgotten, rejected, and abandoned. Self-rejection is the greatest enemy of the spiritual life because it contradicts the sacred voice that calls us the Beloved. Being the Beloved constitutes the core truth of our existence." Nouwen, Henry. Life of the Beloved: Spiritual Living in a Secular World. New York: Crossroad Publishing Company, 2007.

THE ROOT OF SELF-PROTECTION

We all have a deep need not only to be secure but also to feel secure. Rejection will become threatening and hostile to this sense of security so some kind of inner protection becomes essential. However rejected people self-protect out of a wrong motive, fear, which drives them to run and hide. Self-protection is also known as fear of rejection. Fear is always around the corner when rejection affects a person. Past hurts can cause an inability to respond appropriately, and the fear of additional hurt will create defence barriers that prove difficult to get through. The real person becomes not only hidden, but also trapped. It is possible to build self-protection like castles and live in the highest and farthest tower; they dig moats and fill them with sharks and ferocious piranha fish, pull up the drawbridge and declare no one is going to reject them ever again. It is easy to feel safe behind those thick walls; lonely and isolated, not being aware that self-protection is only a deception and a delusion. It is never a long-term solution because eventually we have to let someone in. Jesus is the one who really understands because He has been through it and became victorious over it. He did, and we can, in His name.

Self-Protection And Control

We all have the right to control our lives and destiny including rejected people but rejection only gives rise to distorted reactions and decisions.

- "I will not let people get too close to me because I'm afraid of rejection, failure and betrayal."
- "I will put the barriers up and the shutters down. It is safer to be alone."
- "I will control my own life for no one is going to get close enough to damage me again."
- "I know friendship requires disclosure and sharing of heart; that it too much for me so I will keep my distance and, if necessary, back away even more."

Is it possible to have a more difficult time with the fear of rejection than rejection itself? Fear of rejection is the abdication of power and control over oneself. The person who operates out of a fear of rejection ends up pushing away the very friends, family and helpers who care for him or her and want to help. This will become a cycle of behavior with the same negative results. Someone has said, "fear stands for Forget Everything And Run."

MASKS

Rejected people learn to wear masks to hide what they are really feeling, because they have problems with identity and self-worth. Masks do not protect; they hide.

- The mask of independence - I do not need anyone; I will not be vulnerable.
- The mask of performance - I will do anything to achieve, I will work hard and then you will like me.
- The mask of people pleasing - I will do anything to be accepted; I will do whatever you want me to.
- The mask of fear - I cannot or will not reveal who I really am.

We need to bear in mind that some of these areas will be affected by demonic powers. Help will be needed to discern what is emotional, mindset or the demonic.

THE FRUIT OF REJECTION

It is important to consider the fruit of rejection. The fruit is varied and in some cases considerable, particularly as the roots strengthen and the tree grows.

What Is Fruit?

Fruit can be defined as the product or result of something sown. As a seed is sown, it will root into the ground and ultimately produce, usually above ground a fruit, consisting of a body with a seed in it. Rejection produces fruit and it is important to understand and recognise it. It can be easy to identify the fruit and deal with it, without touching the root. The problem develops when the fruit returns, so is essential to deal with the root as well as pick the fruit.

The fruit of rejection is all about understanding and identifying behaviour and attitudes, reactions and feelings.

Reactions

A reaction is a particular response to a certain situation. With rejection, reaction comes in two forms. These areas are important to understand because the roots of rejection will be seen in either or both of these ways.

Outwardly Or Visible

The response can be over emotional, behaving inappropriately in excitement, noise, angry and aggressive in attitude. Rejected people sometimes defend themselves by attacking others verbally.

Hidden Or Internal

There may be a controlled suppression of the emotions that can be like a dam. Memories can be hidden for many years but still have an effect. Rejected people often escape into themselves because they find it hard to cope with reality. It seems easier to hide and not communicate honestly.

In both areas the response is unconscious. People do not often know why they react as they do, which makes them feel guilty or confused. The real person is rarely seen, which will affect identity and role.

Simple Test

In order to consider the various fruits of rejection, which would explain the root or roots of rejection a person may have, visit Appendix 1 and take the simple test.

MEMORY POINTS

- Trees have roots. Rejection has roots: rebellion, self-rejection and self-protection or fear of rejection.
- Tree roots can cause much damage; roots of rejection will have the same effect.
- Seeds, roots, tree then fruit. As you deal with the roots, the fruit will die.
- Understanding control is vital in the context of rejection.
- Even though the three roots of rejection are so different, there is often an overlap of all three.
- It is important to consider what demonic influence, if any, affects the rejected person.
- People with rejection are good at denial and transferring blame to anyone or anything rather than taking personal responsibility.
- Remember masks.
- The fruit of rejection will only be dealt with effectively when the roots are destroyed.

A Man & A Tree

The story of Zaccheus known to so many, highlights the three roots of rejection; rebellion, self-rejection and self-protection. It is amazing how this man got into a position where he was so despised. He seemed to isolate himself in his anger and pain and took a job that everyone would condemn, a tax collector! He was also the 'chief' tax collector and worked to extract money for the occupying forces, the Romans, which did not go down well at all. Besides this he was a short man and this plays a key part in Zaccheus finding Jesus.

Jesus was passing through Jericho and the story focuses on one man, Zaccheus (Luke 19:1-9). What do we usually think of when we hear Jericho mentioned? Probably the famous battle, where Joshua led the Israelites into a miraculous victory as they went into the Promised Land (Joshua 6).

Jericho means the place of fragrance and was a walled city in the middle of a huge grove of palm trees and had a reputation of being the strongest fortress in Canaan, making it a key to taking the Promised Land. As we may remember God gave the city into the hands of the Israelites in a remarkable manner – the walls fell down!

As Jericho was situated close to the Jordan, in all probability the inhabitants would have known about the miracle of the river Jordan opening up like the Red Sea and the children of Israel walking across on dry land (Josh 3:14-17). They may even have seen the whole event happen.

THE JERICHO CONDITION

In the context of rejection there is a connection to Jericho, which is a key to its understanding. *'Now Jericho was securely shut up because of the children of Israel; none went out, and none came in'* (Joshua 6:1), which means Jericho was shut as tight as the skin of a drum and completely sealed, making it totally secured.

Jericho's walls had the reputation of being impregnable. The walls you build in self-protection become so secure they actually become a prison. This can be defined as an emotional lockdown. You are afraid to reach out or let anyone in. Those with rejection are so good at keeping people out that they have problems letting God in.

Believing you can do everything in your life with the walls up is a fallacy. It is misleading and deceptive making you feel that you are trapped. Your perception is you cannot get out and nobody can get in. "It does not matter what happens to me, the walls will keep me secure."

The fact is that we need an outlet for our emotional pain and if it is not released appropriately, what happens to it? The reality is that it stays and builds up inside to ultimately volcanic proportions, and the emotions will in time go out of control.

FRAGRANCE

At the celebration of Lazarus being raised from the dead (John 12:1-8), Mary, his sister, took an alabaster box of pure spikenard, which was a precious and costly perfume, worth it is said a year's wage. Mary broke the seal of the box and poured the nard over Jesus' head. The whole house was filled with the fragrance of the perfume. Then she poured the nard over his feet and wiped them with her hair.

It was an act of deep thankfulness and worship for her brother's life. She gave everything, the most valuable thing she had. She wanted to show her love toward Jesus and that expression filled the house. She also acted prophetically in preparing him for his coming death. She anointed him for burial. Mary needed to break open the container to release the fragrance and some people there misunderstood the consequences.

If Jericho means fragrance surely the walls need to come down to release it. The defeat of Jericho was a miraculous victory and opened the way into Canaan for further victories. We all have within us the glorious potential of releasing something of the fragrance of God, yet our own walls restrict that. However, if our walls are broken down, something of God's presence will be released. The fragrance of Mary's sacrificial gift to Jesus touched everyone in the house in an overwhelming and beautiful way. This is the miracle and we can be part of it. The fragrance of God will be released from our brokenness.

Broken but healed. Healed but broken. This is the goal for rejected people.

Zacchaeus

Zacchaeus was such a contradiction! His name means clean and pure. How did he cope with that, with the sort of life he led? Zacchaeus, even though he was living a lie, was looking for the reality of unconditional acceptance.

His way of life underlines the issues of rejection:

- He was a tax collector. Tax collectors were despised and hated for working for the oppressive Roman Empire.

- He was the chief tax collector. What did he do to gain that position?
- He was a thief, he was corrupt and he extorted from the people and stole the profits.
- He was wealthy but he was ignored and rejected.
- He was short. Why was that mentioned? Surely it was significant in the sense of how he saw himself, and how other people saw him, and I believe that many rude comments were made to and about him.
- He reacted to the crowd in anger. It seems that he didn't like people and they certainly did not like him. Why would they let him, the chief tax collector, a man loathed and despised, get to the front of the crowd to see Jesus.

There is obviously an undisclosed part of Zacchaeus' life, which deeply influenced him. He is a clear example of a man living with rejection and this is seen in the three roots of rejection:

Self-rejection - He was very small and appeared to be very unhappy with who he was, because he was very short. He saw himself as different and he did not like it.

Fear of rejection and self-protection would have been powerful so he isolated himself, was angry and antagonistic with the people and extracted revenge in his job as a tax collector. Yet as with many who know rejection he was motivated and driven by fear. He could not fail and he certainly could not let people see he was lonely and isolated and no doubt depressed. So he put the walls up and got on with his life by putting himself first and hurting anyone who got in his way.

Rebellion - As the boss he was able to control his staff and the people who could not pay their taxes. He was powerful and used this control and dominance to spread fear. He probably had the power to imprison others. No wonder they hated him.

How did he see himself? What about childhood issues with family and friends? What would have happened when his friends suddenly had growth spurts? Perhaps he became the butt of their jokes and felt rejected, which in turn made him despise who he was. Maybe his mother overprotected him because he was smaller than other children. It is possible that reactive anger began at that time.

All of this is supposition but it is not difficult to come to the conclusion that Zacchaeus was a misfit and lost! Rejected people struggle as to who they are and where they are going; their self-awareness and self-confidence is undermined and it becomes easier to be selfish in the pressure to get the best out of life.

DESIRE

In spite of all of this there was something that made Zacchaeus want to find out about this man Jesus.

- He had heard about Jesus and His miracles.
- We know *"faith comes by hearing"* (Romans 10:17) and something of eternity was stirring within him (Ecclesiastes 3:11), urging him to get to where Jesus was.
- He must have had some questions: "Was he who he said he was?" "Is this a man who could possibly help me?" "Were the stories true about healing?"
- He was desperate enough to do anything to get to Jesus, even climb a tree to see Him.

We are made to respond to God and are not fulfilled until we do.

A MAN UP A TREE

Zacchaeus heard that Jesus was close by, so he ran from his office and into the crowd. He could not see! No doubt he asked, even demanded, and tried to push his way to the front. He could not see; he was too short. All he received was a hostile reaction from the crowd. They did not want a man like him there. No doubt Zacchaeus became more angry as the hassle and banter became too intense and they probably pushed him away. They hated him. So he ran ahead hoping he could find a space. He did not give up even though the odds were really against him.

Do not give up rejected people.

There was no way he could see Jesus, so what was he to do? In his despair he had a crazy idea. He saw a tree and thought to himself, "I could see him from up there." It was an amazing position; he had the best view and was no doubt proud of his achievement, and certainly pleased that he had got one over on the very unfriendly and angry crowd, who were now reacting against him because they realised he had the best view. How remarkable it was that Zacchaeus had yet again turned something around to his advantage.

The imagery here is significant. Those with rejection know about trees. In fact they are up their own trees! They live in a sense of isolation, loneliness, pain and abandonment. They feel no one can help them. They have learned to look after themselves. "So I will protect myself and not let anyone get too close to me. In fact I will live up my tree away from people, control my own life and control the way I relate to others." "I do not like myself, I hate the way I look and I despise so much about me." "I will choose to get away from people because I know if I allow people to get close to me, they will only hurt me and I cannot keep letting that happen." "I can be the life and soul of what is going on, the centre of attention, but no one will know how I really feel."

Trees are significant today even in Christian circles. Being up a tree brings false security. It is deceptive and will cause further pain. People who live in denial usually deny it. It is easier to say to people, "you do not understand me and you do not care, so I will do what I want!"

The words of Jesus can become very challenging to those who are hurting and just want to isolate themselves (Matthew 22:37-39).

- *"Love God with your heart, soul and mind."*
- *"Love your neighbour."*
- *"Love yourself."*

If you do not love and accept yourself, how can you love your neighbour and how can you love God? We are made for relationship and community and not to live up a tree, away from everyone and everything, in a self-protecting and isolating manner. Jesus' words are unmistakable for these two commandments are foundational to all that the law and prophets have said!. It cannot get any clearer that.

Being up your own tree of rejection, independent of everyone else, only feeds the hurt and pain. Maybe it is time to come down and face reality and, as we will see, Jesus in his compassion, care and love will be there waiting for you.

A TIME FOR CONFRONTATION

As much as possible Zaccheus had settled himself up his tree, as the crowd became silent, because Jesus was getting closer. There is always a time to be confronted with the claims of Jesus and thankfully our God is more than a God of the second chance. He will keep bringing you back to the point of decision to change.

It was Zaccheus' time and the opportunity was given in quite a surprising way. Suddenly Jesus stopped under the tree, looked up and spoke. Imagine Zaccheus trying to hide behind the leaves and branches in a mixture of shock, fear and astonishment. The amazing thing is Jesus called him by name. It seems it was one of those incredible revelations of knowledge that Jesus often had. Maybe Zaccheus almost fell out of the tree in shock!

He Knows Us By Name

Jesus knew his name although He had not met him before. No one had introduced them. Nathaniel said to Jesus, *"how do you know me?"* (John 1:48) Jesus knew and we may debate how, but the point is Jesus knew. It shows He cared; it shows He wants relationship and it shows He wants to help.

Before we were born God knew us (Jeremiah 1:5). God said, *"fear not for I have redeemed you; I have called you by name, you are mine"* (Isaiah 43:1). It gives us confidence if He knows our name for He must know all about us and yet, He still reaches out to us to come down from our trees. His great and wonderful love unconditionally accepts us.

When Jesus said, *"I need to stay at your house today"* He was showing Zacchaeus He wanted relationship not just obedience.

- Jesus was not going to climb the tree and have a pity party, sitting on a branch. He wanted Zaccheus to come down. It was a sign of humility and obedience.
- Jesus wanted Zaccheus' personal response acknowledging Him and making a choice to obey Him.

There is a challenge here for us. Jesus wants a response. He does not just want us to come down from the tree: He wants the tree to be cut down once and for all so that there is nowhere to hide.

Zaccheus must have been shocked but he responded because he saw the personableness of Jesus. He speaks to us as individuals, as friends, because he knows us, loves us and certainly accepts us as Zaccheus quickly found out.

The crowd murmured and muttered but Zaccheus took no notice and welcomed Jesus gladly. Jesus had invited himself and all Zaccheus had to do was to accept and take Jesus home. Zaccheus had a change of heart and took the initiative; Jesus did not have to tell him what to do. In repentance Zacchaeus returned more than the law required and gave half of his possessions to the poor. This is restitution; the sign of being forgiven. Zaccheus put things right. This is Jesus reaching out to the neglected, despised and rejected.

LOST OR FOUND?

Jesus said something amazing to Zaccheus when He said, *"today salvation has come to this house! This man is a son of Abraham. For the Son of Man came to seek and to save that which was lost"* (Luke 19:9-10).

- Salvation - the word means immediate deliverance and is a form of the Old Testament word meaning Jesus. Zaccheus by birth is a son of Abraham. However being a tax collector he was considered by the people to be a traitor, a heathen and everyone despised him, just as they despised the Gentiles, yet his change of heart brought him into a great freedom as he responded to Jesus.
- This house - Although his whole family was obviously affected when Jesus came to the house, Jesus had come to Zaccheus personally and he truly believed.
- Son of Abraham - Zaccheus, although not worthy received Jesus through repentance and showed he had faith just like Abraham and therefore, a right to enter into the kingdom of God.

- Seek - We need to realise that as much as God wants us to seek Him, He is always seeking us as a Shepherd with His sheep.
- Save the lost - lost in this context means being in the wrong place rather than being doomed. Someone is lost when they are away from God and is found when they find their right place with God.

Rejected people who are 'restless wanderers' can be found. There is hope.

"You shall know the truth and the truth shall set you free" (John 8:32).

MEMORY POINTS

- The life of Zaccheus highlights the three areas of rejection: rebellion, self-rejection and self-protection.
- The Jericho condition - emotional lockdown.
- Jericho the place of fragrance.
- Zaccheus, a contradiction; Maybe we are more like him than we realise.
- His desire to see Jesus took him right out of his comfort zone and up a tree.
- Rejected people like trees.
- Amazingly Jesus confronted Zaccheus, called him by his name and invited himself to his home.
- Zaccheus had a change of heart, which Jesus honoured.
- Salvation came.
- The lost can be found.

Causes - Part 1

Traumatic events at any time in a person's life can cause deep wounding. Depending on the severity of the issue and how it is handled, it is possible for a root of rejection to be established.

The effect is the consequence of the cause. The emotional response to a traumatic experience is not predictable. One dear woman we met never recovered from the loss of her son in a tragic accident. Time seemed to stop for her and her grief remained evident. Many years have passed and she has not been able to move on. My mother-in-law also lost a son in tragic circumstances. She found God in that terrible time and seemed to move on as well as we could hope. It was only when she was facing death, through cancer, that she told us she had always had flashbacks, nightmares and night terrors relating to that time. In the first example, the effect of the trauma remained evident. The second one shows it was buried and stayed hidden, deep in the unconscious part of the mind. You never bury your problems dead.

It is important to look at the reasons and grounds for rejection for they will influence and affect us even in the womb. How we respond to things that happen to us through our lives are like seeds from which the roots and fruit of rejection grow.

There is a vast difference between a reason for feeling rejected and an excuse for feeling rejected. It is easy to blame others for what has happened but learning to take responsibility for personal actions and reactions will lead to a greater sense of freedom even though it is a challenge.

CHILDREN

Babies are emotional beings right from birth. It is believed that they are born with basic emotions, which are the stepping-stones to their emotional development. A child is hungry for love and his emotions will develop in a secure manner if his parents genuinely love him and are clearly connected. This will have a nurturing effect on the child. Parents have a responsibility to love unconditionally and without expectation, which in turn will have a positive effect on the child's ongoing development, which is the right sort of attachment leading to strong bonding.

Unconditional love is about a parent meeting the emotional needs of the child. Emotionally deficient love may lead to insecurity and anxiety, which is emotional deprivation. All of this sows the seeds of rejection, particularly as rejection basically means, 'you have no value' for this is what the child will hear. This is different to a child who has security in his parent's unconditional love.

Rejection undermines our need to belong. We all have a fundamental need to belong. In rejection this need becomes destabilised and the disconnection the child feels adds to the emotional pain. The child will feel alone and isolated.

It is clear that young children cannot take responsibility for their own actions, but as they develop mentally and emotionally, their parents will show them, in measure, how to do that. This takes time but it is possible to train a child in this way. It is clear though, as we shall see, that the child even in the womb is an aware human being and is therefore vulnerable to causes of rejection. It is usually in adulthood that these issues surface and can be dealt with. It is then that the challenge to take personal responsibility comes into focus because blaming someone else can only foster further rejection.

No love, no value; no value, no love...

CONCEPTION

Rejection can begin in the form of a wound, hurt or demonic oppression before a child is born. Many adults have found that the roots of their problems have been sourced in childhood or even earlier, in the womb. Bonding begins to take place at this time with both parents and if, for example, the father is missing rejection may begin to affect the child.

'We now know that the unborn child is an aware, reacting human being who from the sixth month on (and perhaps earlier) leads an active emotional life. Along with this startling finding we have made the following discoveries:

a)   The foetus can see, hear, experience, taste and, on a primitive level, even learn in utero (that is in the uterus before birth). Most importantly, he can feel not with an adult's sophistication, but feel nonetheless.

b)   A corollary to this discovery is that what a child feels and perceives begins shaping his attitudes and expectations about himself. Whether he ultimately sees himself and, hence, acts as a happy or sad, aggressive or meek, secure or anxiety ridden person depends, in part, on the messages he gets about himself in the womb' (Verney and Kelly. The Secret Life of the Unborn Child. London: Sphere Books, 1982).

Therefore it is clear that denial of love can affect a child before it is born. The womb becomes the child's first home. Is it friendly or unfriendly, peaceful or hostile? The child will receive both parents' feelings and thoughts. Their attitude and relationship with the child before it is born will affect it after it is born.

The following may be reasons for rejection before birth:
- An unwanted pregnancy.
- Illegitimacy carried a stigma and had consequences until quite recently. There is a reference in scripture to a curse of ten generations (Deuteronomy 23:2). This can be cut off in Jesus name. It is possible for conception outside of marriage to produce a demonic oppression of poverty, uncleanness and insecurity. However in this context unconditional love can be a buffer to the enemy.
- The family is already too large.
- A mistake. Many adults carry this and are weighed down by it. It is as if they have a sticker saying this on their foreheads for everyone to see. It can produce a lack of attachment or bonding, which will lead to a sense of abandonment and isolation later in life. There is no doubt I was a mistake particularly as my mother was married to another man. The problems caused dramatically affected me but I am so thankful to God, my loving Heavenly Father for healing me. By the way my parents kept me.
- Financial problems.
- Conception too soon after marriage.
- Fear of the birth, fear of deformity.
- Attempted abortion.
- Babies born to women who have become pregnant through, rape, incest, adultery or mothers who were alcoholics or dependant on drugs.
- Separation or divorce before the baby was born. Sometimes the child will be blamed.

- A shock or trauma during pregnancy, such as an accident or the death of someone in the family or a close friend.
- The mother becoming pregnant at quite a late age.
- Miscarriage of a previous child.
- A premature birth.

It is good to know however, that God is very concerned about children in the womb and scripture is so encouraging and comforting:

- *"You made all the delicate, inner parts of my body and knit me together in my mother's womb. Thank you for making me so wonderfully complex! Your workmanship is marvelous - how well I know it. You watched me as I was being formed in utter seclusion, as I was woven together in the dark of the womb. You saw me before I was born. Every day of my life was recorded in your book. Every moment was laid out before a single day had passed"* (Psalm 139:13-16 NLT).
- *"I have called you by your name, you are mine"* (Isaiah 43:1).
- *"Before I was born the Lord called me; from my birth He made mention of my name"* (Isaiah 49:1 NIV).
- *"Before I formed you in the womb I knew you"* (Jeremiah 1:5).
- *'Chosen before the foundation of the world'* (Ephesians 1:4).
- *'We are His workmanship'* (Ephesians 2:10).

God has a great sense of love and care for us even before we are born and although He sees the pain, He will bring healing as we respond to Him.

The mystery is that He knew us before we were born.
- He knew us.
- He knew our name.
- He chose us.
- He called us.
- We are His workmanship, His works of art.

This is acceptance, closeness, this is value and this is love. This is God, our God and if He thinks this about me, I want to follow Him and give Him everything. There is no better way of responding to and receiving healing than to realise God thinks about rejected people like this.

Note: Some of the examples given reflect the circumstances of a different generation and it needs to be borne in mind that medical and social care has advanced since then. The principles however remain the same.

The Birth

It is clear that rejection can be caused by the actual birth or soon afterwards.

- The pain, pressure, isolation and loneliness of a long birth can put the mother, and even the father under great mental pressure. Sometimes things can be said that are later regretted.
- The opposite can also affect the child. The shock of a fast delivery or a caesarean birth or a birth with instruments.
- Some babies need special attention at birth or immediate surgery. An emergency that takes the baby away from its mother, so that suddenly he is out of his secure environment without any bonding and is put in an incubator.
- Other babies may need further attention and have to stay in hospital for a prolonged period of time while the mother goes home. The strength of bonding is tested and any separation can cause a sense of abandonment. It is as though the baby becomes a victim of circumstances beyond its parent's control.
- The mother's death at the birth of her baby.
- After being born, the baby was immediately taken away and adopted.
- Feeding problems caused by fear, insecurity or medical problems.
- If the mother or father or both have known rejection, it is probable the baby will. How parents show love, acceptance and affection is important.

- Sex preference can be a serious issue for some parents. If both or one of the parents show disappointment in the sex of their child, it is possible there may be problems in the future. The child may take the disappointment on board and feel guilty and rejected. What if the couple felt 'the Lord' had shown them the sex of the child and they got it wrong. The child may ultimately come to hate and reject itself and even try to be the opposite sex in order to please mum or dad. It is possible for this to lead to gender confusion.
- Children born deformed or disfigured.
- Not naming a child for a long time. I know of a child that was not named for 6 months!
- Being a replacement child. Conceived because a sibling died. Some parents would even give the child the same name.
- Parents or doctors not realising that there was a second baby in the womb.
- Anaesthetic - baby had to fight to be born because the mother was asleep.
- A surviving twin.

INFANCY

Rejection may also affect a child as it is growing up. The first few months and years of a child's life are foundational and formative. Young children have no clear picture of who they are. They see themselves in the mirror of their parent's evaluation. If a child is repeatedly told they are stupid, no good, etc, they will act accordingly. Their spirits are wide open for influence from those who are close and they will reflect both the positive and negative. Babies seem to know those who are safe, but in their vulnerability cannot guard themselves against those who are not safe. What is spoken into them will affect them in the future.

- Words affect children, i.e. "you were a mistake", "we did not want any children", "we did not want you, we wanted a boy or girl" and "I wish you had never been born". Life and death is in the power of the tongue (Proverbs 18:21).
- Children are easily embarrassed by being constantly reminded that they look like their mother or have grandfathers nose or squint like their brother. This can cause problems with self-image.
- Sometimes children are separated too early in life for far too long from their parents. However legitimate this separation is, the child may be affected.
- Some children adopted in their early months or years have been known to have symptoms of rejection, despite being brought up in a caring and loving family.
- Fostering, sometimes going to many different homes.
- Preferential treatment of one child over others can cause rejection. It may cause attention seeking and friction.
- The trauma or shock of death, divorce or separation. This is perceived rejection and is as powerful as actual rejection.
- Physical disabilities, learning disabilities and other special needs.
- Prolonged childhood illness or hospitalisation can bring isolation.
- The way parents talk, confront, argue in front of their children, can bring insecurity and ultimately rejection. Children blame themselves easily.

School Life And Teenage Years

In the very important years leading up to adulthood, there are many changes and decisions to face. Experiences at school have an enormous effect on a child's sense of worth and self-image.

The following points show some of the incidents that can feed rejection:
- Children over criticised, over disciplined, dominated, ignored or even favoured over the others will be open to rejection.

- Being sent to boarding school, some at a very early age.
- Moving house many times and often at critical points in the child's studies. This includes the pressure of, yet again, feeling lonely and having to make new friends.
- Being bullied and unfairly treated by teachers or other children. For example, being ridiculed because you do not like sport.
- Embarrassing incidents or being misunderstood at school, which can lead to self-image problems.
- Parents putting on their children a pressure to succeed and making sure they pass exams with the best marks, which may lead to guilt, perfectionism and self-rejection.
- Disinterest of parents in schoolwork.
- Religious pressure on children from parents can cause legalism, traditionalism and inflexibility, which will lead to self-rejection.
- Self-criticisms need to be taken seriously as they are inner vows (see Roots and Fruit chapter). Remember they are promises we make to ourselves. They are powerful and can be difficult to dislodge.
- Exclusion from group of friends. Being called names.
- Being laughed at in school.
- Being ridiculed for not understanding what is being taught.
- Being devalued in school or home, not allowed to have an opinion.
- Constant sickness causing academic problems will affect self-worth.
- The start of long-term chronic illness in teenage years may cause problems related to rejection.
- Injustice at being punished wrongly.
- A teacher always favouring or picking on a student.
- Pressure from parents because brother or sister has done better.
- Guilt over a teenage pregnancy, sexual experience or abortion.
- Undiagnosed dyslexia causing learning difficulties, frustration and criticism.
- Unusual physical features, either birth defect or family trait, which causes embarrassment, teasing and name-calling. This

includes children with disabilities such as those in wheelchairs even though so much is done to help a child feel integrated. The issue is being different and this can cause feelings of isolation.

- Racism.
- Religious intolerance.
- Sexual intolerance.

FAMILY REJECTION

What goes on within the family is so important in the development of relationships between parents and children. There is so much that can cause the roots of rejection. Many people have suffered in this way.

- Constant criticism in the family.
- Poverty in the family.
- Immigration difficulties i.e. language, racism. Often children are in the forefront of the problem of translation, etc.
- Speech difficulty in family, e.g. stuttering.
- Reading or spelling difficulties e.g. dyslexia.
- Domination by one member of the family.
- Being made fun of by family members because of embarrassing personal features.
- Cruel parents.
- Unhappy parents.
- An absent father. He may be doing legitimate work but not being there, is not meeting the needs of his child.
- Promises that are consistently broken create a lack of trust.
- Alcohol or any other addiction in the family.
- Embarrassment over religious beliefs.
- A family member convicted of a crime.
- Parents showing no active interest or giving any time to the development of the child.

- Lack of affection in the family, i.e. "we don't talk about things like love", "we are not a demonstrative family", "we get embarrassed."
- Redundancy or long periods of unemployment.
- Financial disasters.
- Homelessness.
- Separation, broken engagement or divorce.
- Sexual abuse whether inside or outside the family.
- Feeling physically unattractive.
- Sexual dysfunction in the family.
- Being ashamed of one's gender.
- A refusal to have sexual relations in marriage.
- Unfaithfulness in the marriage.
- An inability to have children.
- Lack of intimacy in the family.
- An inability to communicate by either or both parents. It is vital to talk, to show by action that you care and love one another.
- Being forced into adult responsibilities in childhood or teenage years.
- Ill-treatment by step parents.
- Being forced by parents into wrong behaviour, i.e. stealing, immorality.
- Neglect in childhood.
- The premature death of parents or any other member of the family.
- Being an only child and over protected.
- Being a middle or youngest child and ignored.
- Being the eldest child with unrealistic expectations put on you.
- Feeling responsible for a dysfunctional parent.
- Coping with the fact that you have been adopted and you do not know your real parents.
- Children that are fostered might express rejection.
- Being a disabled person.
- Having a learning disability.
- Children rejecting their parents especially when they are old.

- Evacuation in war.
- Sport or music at weekends with parent's showing no commitment.
- Parents being too busy in Christian work.

MEMORY POINTS

- Rejection has a cause and an effect.
- The cause produces a response from within, which may become a trauma or wound, an area where rejection can take hold.
- It is remarkable to see how extensively rejection can affect someone.
- Remember you never bury your problems dead however deep they may be.
- A child can be affected by rejection even in the womb.
- Children are born with needs that parents' unconditional love can meet.
- Genuine love develops emotions.
- Emotionally deficient love will produce emotional depravation and the seeds of rejection will be sown.
- Rejection can begin in the womb and continue throughout the person's life.
- God has known us from before we were born and He has always been with us. Because of this we can be secure in His love and acceptance.

CAUSES - PART 2

In the world today probably the greatest desire is for a society with peace and harmony in every area of life. The underlying philosophy of most political systems is to create a world that exists for the benefit of all; no disease, no shortage of food, no crime and peaceful relations for all humanity.

The reality is that this has not happened and what we see is entropy, a growth of chaos from a gradual decline of disorder. We see an exposure of pain, hurt and damage both in families on a national and international scale.

One area affecting many individuals that consistently damages mentally, emotionally, physically and spiritually is abuse. So much more has been exposed recently that indicates what has been hidden not only in families, but also in other areas of society where you would not have thought abuse could happen even the church.

As human beings, we have a strong need to feel secure. Abuse makes a person vulnerable to the three roots of rejection; rebellion, self-rejection and self-protection whether as a cause or as a consequence. This will make the person feel they have no worth and this will bring feelings of insecurity, abandonment, fearfulness and hopelessness. Abuse means betrayal, which is a violation of trust bringing conflict and division in a relationship.

Abuse is defined as any action that intentionally harms, injures or insults another person. Its essence is the mental or physical mistreatment of a person, frequently resulting in serious emotional, mental, physical, and/or sexual injury.

- To use wrongly, to exploit, to mistreat.
- To be cruel.
- To inflict physical, sexual, or psychological harm.
- To use insulting, coarse, or bad language about or to someone.

Rejection can be intentional, which can be defined as emotional abuse in its most simple form. It also wounds a person's spirit, sometimes slightly, but those wounds can also be deep and very painful. Unhealthy, abusive relationships are damaging particularly to children.

As we consider the different types of abuse, it is important to remember that this can happen from birth to old age. Abuse causes rejection and rejection causes abuse.

When a person is used to something happening consistently however bad it is, to them it is part of normal life. This can make it hard to understand that what is happening is wrong.

LAURA

I met Laura through a dear Baptist minister, who became a very good friend to Chris and I in the mid 1980's. She was pastoring in a difficult area in the west of the city. Laura was in her mid twenties and looked very pretty and had beautiful eyes. However as I got to know her I saw that her eyes became a powerful tool in her ability to control, manipulate, seduce, and at times show anger and hatred.

Laura was a very damaged young lady but you would probably not be aware of this, as she hid things well and was very charming. She had an eating disorder and predisposition to self-harm rooted in an abusive family experience. Self-harm was also the fruit of other abuse. She was full of anger and rage and would sometimes think nothing of throwing chairs around the waiting room of the doctor's surgery and at the rehabilitation centre. At one time she was banned from the surgery and her day centre because of her violence and the damage she caused. Sometimes she was sectioned and placed in a secure hospital or residential centre for several weeks. I have no doubt these times were very helpful to her, although some relationships with other patients were mutually damaging and abusive.

The roots of rejection were exposed through her angry, sometimes sullen and depressive rebellion and through self-hate with frequent proclamation of wanting to kill herself. This also included an obsessive need to protect herself, particularly by not wanting to or being able to trust. Laura was a paradox. She was crying out for attention, yet as people attempted to get close to her she rejected them. All this was rooted in emotional, verbal and sexual abuse as a child and as a young woman. There was no doubt too that Laura in her rejection was very capable of giving verbal and emotional abuse to others.

She was a complicated young woman and was referred to a consultant psychiatrist. It was not too long after I got to know Laura that I was introduced to her psychiatrist who wanted to meet me. Laura had told her about some of the positive aspects of prayer that she had received and this led to me to meet this really nice and approachable devout Catholic who specialised in eating disorders and was aware of the area of healing in the scriptures. I prayed a number of times for Laura with her psychiatrist present.

Over the years Laura improved and she began to integrate into our Church Fellowship. She worked with one of the church administrators and I still have study and sermon notes typed by her. This was a good season for her and we did wonder whether there would be complete healing. It became very difficult for a while when Laura went through a stage of dependency on Chris and I and there was an obsession to relate to me as her father. This was sorted out peaceably but I know that overriding need was later transferred to a medical person. Her former Baptist Pastor came under similar pressure particularly with many, many phone calls day and night. We had to set boundaries, which were not well received and finally things drifted.

I do recall one Sunday evening Laura walking in after the church service had started with blood running down her arms and a half empty bottle of strong cider in her hand. She walked down the aisle of the packed church to the front row and everybody saw her. She did make an impression! Laura attempted to visit other churches in the city without much success, although she did eventually stay at one very good church. By that time we had moved 200 miles north. She actually did pretty well and what we heard was that she was integrating into church again.

In the years we saw Laura we attempted to deal with her abuse and the consequences of that through a mix of prayer ministry, pastoral care and friendship and saw some blessing. I continued to work with Laura's psychiatrist and we even saw some deliverance and inner healing. Even the psychiatrist was pleased at her improvement. Long after we had moved north we heard she had dropped out of most everything and began to isolate herself, ultimately becoming a lonely figure once again.

A few years ago we heard the shocking news that Laura had tragically died. The funeral was a very sad occasion as she was committed to the Lord.

The area that we had no knowledge about back there related to the hurt child. Through the pain of abuse it was probable that Laura dissociated and the wounded and damaged little girl remained hidden within the broken woman. As far as I can see there was no healing leading to a peaceable integration, which would have been one of the keys in her ultimate healing.

There is no condemnation or guilt because we all did what we could with a precious life and learned so much through it. We know Laura is with her Lord in complete wholeness. We will never forget her...

Emotional And Verbal Abuse In Children And Adults

Emotional abuse is any form of mental or emotional control on another person, verbally or non-verbally. It is clear that adults as well as children can on the one hand be wounded by cruel, malicious and harsh words or on the other by the mental and emotional pressure of being deliberately ignored. A further definition of emotional abuse is, 'any act including confinement, isolation, verbal assault, humiliation, intimidation or any other treatment which may diminish the sense of identity, dignity, and self-worth.' Therefore people who suffer from emotional abuse will be affected by low self-esteem and this will contribute to a personality change as they become withdrawn, depressive and anxious.

Emotional abuse is an act of bringing fear and intimidation to another person, which will ultimately lead to control over them. Over a period of time it slowly eats away at a victim's self-confidence until they feel they can no longer trust, not only anyone else, but possibly even themselves as they lose their sense of self-worth. It is a type of indoctrination as it creates a belief system, which will lead to certain behaviour patterns, relating to protection of self. If you lose confidence through another's abuse, you will want to create a lifestyle of protection, which may show outwardly with certain behaviour such as an obedient or subservient attitude. It can also be completely hidden within the unconscious. If you are told you are useless and not good for anything, you will find that the words will affect you and create a mind-set. This will lead you to behave accordingly instead of in that way and you may find yourself thinking and speaking those negative words to yourself.

Abuse by adults happens when someone misuses their authority to mistreat someone else. This happens in every area in society, basically wherever people are. Often the perpetrator is someone who has a position of authority in the workplace. They show no regard or concern for the individual and that authority is used to control and manipulate, so that people are put into a submissive or compliant role. It is not difficult to create an unstable relationship in the abuser's favour because they hold the power. The victim will have their confidence undermined and will believe it is their fault and they deserve to be treated that way so they will easily disregard personal worth. Others may relate to a childhood issue they thought they had left behind, but when they find themselves in a similar situation, they may feel that the abuse they suffer is a normal part of life due to what they experienced as a child.

Many abused children cling to the hope that growing up will bring a form of escape and liberty. They think moving away from the situation will change everything. However, it is not only getting out of the abusive environment but also confronting the issue, which will brings healing. If a child's personality has been affected within an environment of control, they will not relate well to adult life. They are still left with their hurts and their basic problems of trust and rejection.

Abuse that takes place in the family environment creates a belief in the child that family is a dangerous place where people hurt each other. The source of their pain could well be their parents, so who will protect them? This perception can bring emotional separation and isolation in the family. The abused child may well either be wrongly blamed or blame themselves. Family secrets can be connected to abuse and become common ground for rejection, particularly when a child is involved. In certain areas the child, just by being in the home, can be a trigger to events that have happened in the past such as an affair, rape, a relationship that has failed or in some other way. The child may have a different father or mother and they become a constant reminder of the problem. It is not difficult to take out the pain of regret, unforgiveness, guilt and anger on the confused child. Parents sometimes live a lie about their marriage because of a pregnancy and deceive the child by not being open. This happened in my own family as my mother became pregnant with me when she was married to another man. Finally she was divorced and married my father a few years later. I found out about the event in my early thirties. This affected me over the years even though I did not know about it. I now know more than ever that God saw me through the trauma of that revelation. Children have been blamed for trapping the parents in a marriage with no love because they wanted to do or were forced into doing 'the right thing.' There may be good reasons, but often it is the child who feels abused and rejected. It seems as though neither parent can allow themselves to love the child.

Parents usually bring their children up in the same way they were brought up. If they were abused and rejected they treat the child in a similar way because that was the only way they knew. They give pain out of their own childhood pain. The problem is we do not choose our parents but we are dependent on them in the early years of our lives. As children we deserve the best our parents can give. In reality that may not happen and we can be left with deep emotional, mental and spiritual wounds. If these scarred areas are not healed, the abused child as an adult may well continue the cycle.

Verbal abuse is a powerful tool of emotional abuse. Someone can be abused by being shouted at, sworn at, and humiliated privately or publically or through constant critical, cruel and unkind words. The abuser may also use silence to cause fear and anxiety by refusing to talk to the victim and acting as if they are not there or do not even exist. The abused person may be threatened with physical violence and therefore constantly live in fear. It is all to do with dominating and controlling a person. Many people suffer verbal and emotional abuse in secret for years, not really understanding what is happening or why they feel so afflicted mentally and emotionally. The abuser is a bully who wants superiority so that they are looked up to but this is rooted in fear and fear of rejection. However, it is often the abuser who has the fear and what they do is to attempt to place their victim in a similar position by making him or her believe the negative things said about them.

A person may be confronted by relational inconsistencies such as an alcoholic parent or spouse who comes home happy one night and angry the next. They will live in confusion and fear for they do not know whom they are going to meet.

Anyone can be verbally abused from childhood through to old age; in the school, the home, the work place or the church. It is usually difficult to gain evidence or visible proof, as most of this happens privately and the abuser is probably always wonderful around others.

Emotional abuse often develops as a cycle. In a relationship, this cycle starts when one partner emotionally abuses the other as they, for various reasons show dominance and control. The abuser feels guilty because of what they have done, but more because of the consequences of their actions. The excuses are then made for their behaviour in order to avoid taking responsibility for what has happened. 'Normal' behaviour then resumes as if the abuse never happened. Anything can be said or done, such as overdoing the charm, giving presents and continually being apologetic in order to make the abused believe the abuser is sorry. Sometime later, something triggers and more emotional abuse takes place.

EXAMPLES OF EMOTIONAL ABUSE

- Aggression such as blaming, demanding, threatening, accusing, criticising, and name-calling or threats of violence or abandonment.
- Intentionally frightening, terrorising and intimidating, creating fear and stress.

- Making an individual fear that they will not receive the food or care they need.
- Lies and deception.
- Making derogative or slanderous statements about an individual to others.
- Socially isolating an individual.
- Isolating a child from family or friends.
- Withholding important information.
- Denying the emotional needs of another by not listening or talking to them.
- Trivialising incidents to make a person feel unimportant.
- Repeatedly raising the issue of death.
- Telling an individual that they are too much trouble.
- Ignoring or excessively criticizing.
- Being over-familiar and disrespectful.
- Treating an individual like a servant.

PHYSICAL ABUSE

Physical abuse is the infliction of physical pain or injury. Although the physical side is horrible, consider the emotional hurt and humiliation that a person suffers through this and how long it may take to heal. Physical abuse can happen to both children and adults of either gender and of any sexual orientation. Physically abused children are at risk of later interpersonal problems involving aggressive behaviour and adolescents are at a much greater risk of substance abuse. In addition, depression, emotional distress, and suicidal thoughts are also symptoms of people who have been physically abused. Many abusive and neglectful parents have had little exposure to positive parental models and support, so the cycle continues into the next generation.

To suffer physical abuse is never the fault of the victim and it may result in self-harm.

SELF-HARM

On the 4th February 1983 one of my favourite singers of all time died. Karen Carpenter was only thirty-two and had already achieved so much in the music world with her effortless velvet voice. She died of a heart condition, which was brought on by anorexia nervosa that developed because Karen abused her body to achieve weight loss.

Anorexia can be defined as a struggle for control. The two things Karen valued most was her voice and her mothers love. Yet she felt desperately unloved by her mother who favoured her brother Richard and it was Richard who took control of her voice, as he was the musical driving force leaving Karen to struggle with low self-esteem. A comment in the media about her 'chubby' appearance when she was seventeen made her determined to seize control of the only thing left and that was her body. She lost considerable weight quickly and this soon became out of her control.

At one time Karen's therapist told the family that Karen really needed to hear that they loved her. Her mother retorted, "We just don't do things that way." As Karen got weaker, she became extremely dehydrated, and other complications led to her collapse and eventual death. The post mortem revealed a drug in her body that she had been secretly taking to make her vomit, but unknowingly over a period of time it had slowly destroyed the heart muscle. In all probability she accidentally killed herself. What a great tragedy.

Self-harm is when somebody intentionally damages or injures their body such as cutting or scratching, causing bruises, banging their head against a wall, pulling out hair, burning and breaking bones. Some types of eating disorder are connected to self-harm. It is a way of coping with or expressing overwhelming emotional distress. Self-harm is when people hurt themselves or damage their health on purpose.

Usually people do this in secret; it is more prevalent than we think. Sometimes when people self-harm they think about death, but often the intention is more to punish themselves, express their distress or relieve unbearable tension. Self-harm can be a cry for help as signs of depression or deep emotional distress are not always evident.

There are lots of reasons why young people might self-harm. The need to hurt themselves usually comes from emotions that are very difficult to cope with.

Self-harm is perceived as a way to release tension. Physical pain is easier to deal with than emotions. It can also be a way of controlling something, especially if they feel that other parts of their life are out of control or they are trapped in a difficult situation.

Self-harm can also be used as a form of self-punishment for something that a person feels bad about. Feeling alone, experiencing low self-esteem and not feeling good enough can also lead to self-harm. It is probably not suicidal in intent but an expression of pain that comes from self-hatred, low self-esteem or guilt. The physical pain brings relief for a while and eventually becomes habit forming.

There are lots of myths about the kind of people who self-harm. It is clear however that self-harm is something that people from all walks of life can struggle with. This does not depend on your sex, age, religion or background.

Everyone has a different trigger for starting to self-harm. Some young people start self-harming after being abused or bullied. It could be a reaction to a stressful event. Other young people self-harm because of pressure to do well at school or because they feel alone. It does not have to be a big thing. An argument or a situation that made them feel embarrassed or left them feeling depressed might lead to someone self-harming. It is an expression of distress whereby the individual is more 'attention needing' rather than 'attention seeking.'

Sexual Abuse

Sexual abuse is when a child or young person is pressurised, forced, tricked or coerced into taking part in any kind of sexual activity with an adult or another young person who is forcefully dominant or significantly older. It creates deep wounding and probably with demonic activity including the various roots and fruit of rejection. Some of the consequences of sexual abuse will include anger and depression, a tendency to hate yourself and a growing ability to protect yourself against further abuse.

Admitting to being a victim of sexual abuse is often suppressed and deeply buried, maybe because the problem lies within the family. If someone in their family abuses a child or young person the guilt, fear and confusion means they will endure the shame because of loyalty or fear of reprisals or threats. There will be negative results in later life whether the person gets married or not. There is always a violation of dignity, sexuality and humanity, which will bring its own problems, especially in marital relationships. The person will grow up with a sense of defilement and will be in conflict with hate, fear and distrust.

Rape is a crime. It is one person forcing another person to have sexual intercourse against their will. Force can mean physical force that overcomes resistance, or intimidation either expressed or implied by abduction or the threat of death. It does not take much to see the emotional, mental and spiritual consequences of rape.

It is important to know that just because the victim did not say no, it does not mean that they meant yes. When someone does not resist an unwanted sexual advance, it does not mean that they are consenting. Sometimes physical resistance can put a victim at a bigger risk of further physical or sexual abuse. Some think that if the victim did not resist, it does not count as abuse. That is not true.

This myth is damaging in its own right because it makes it more difficult for the victim to speak out and more likely that they will blame themselves. Whether they were intoxicated or felt pressured, intimidated or obligated to act a certain way, it is never the victim's fault.

Abuse In Marriage Or A Committed Relationship

Abuse in marriage or a committed relationship is a well-known fact, though through loyalty and fear, it is sometimes more difficult to disclose. Regretfully in today's society and across many cultures there are so many broken families. It is not only one of the partnership who suffers abuse, but the children in that relationship are also deeply affected because they have witnessed the emotional, verbal or physical abuse. The power to control the relationship will be seen through domination and manipulation.

A proportion of children who have witnessed physical violence in their parent's relationship will grow up demonstrating significant behavioural and emotional problems. They will react against marriage or even think that in marriage, "I can get my own way and what I want by being violent. It worked for dad."

Separation and or divorce will probably lead to some form of rejection. Whoever is right or wrong in the situation is not ultimately the problem. It is the reaction and attitude of both parties to the other, and the way they feel about themselves. It is declared in the marriage ceremony, 'whom God has joined, let no man put asunder.' This confession before God, one another and witnesses creates a spiritual bond. The breaking of that bond through separation and/or divorce causes deep wounding and rejection. This can be so difficult for Christian families and church leaders. It is happening though and we need to be aware of the feeling of being cast aside, the worthlessness, the pain and rejection felt, notwithstanding losing income, homes, friends and schools even children losing relationship with one or both parents.

Rejection in marriage can happen without separation or divorce. There may not be any possibility of parting, so the marriage just exists. It can be called 'silent divorce.' When this is happening, some examples of this may include telling a partner they are worthless, and degrading them by name-calling or frequent negative comments about looks or abilities. Ignoring or withholding love or even touch is emotional abuse and will make the victim feel isolated. The abuse may come through the jealousy of one party or of the other. Suffocating a relationship will squeeze the life out of it, as restrictions are demanded when unreal suspicions grow and accusations made.

Being rejected day by day in marriage is destructive and violating to either person. Many get so worn down they do not know which way to turn partly because trust has eroded. Most people face tremendous trials when their spouse becomes violent and abusive.

It is possible the relationship has been in decline for quite a while or it may be that a shocking sudden circumstance happens and all at once there is division leading to separation, a loss of trust and accusations of betrayal. The mix of anger and the pain of depression will be prevalent and the trauma caused will last. No one, under any circumstance, deserves to feel disregarded, insulted, controlled, coerced, intimidated, hurt, hit, pushed, grabbed, or touched in any uninvited way. Nothing that anyone in a family says or does justifies abuse.

Whatever the circumstances it is often apparent that rejection would affect one if not both parties deeply.

SPIRITUAL ABUSE

In the very place where you would think there is safety, the church, there is abuse. There has been in recent times, an exposure of many sexual abuse cases in the church, but spiritual abuse has gone largely unnoticed.

In defining Spiritual Abuse it is important to give a warning. It would be easy to use the term in an irresponsible way to feed a personal agenda and lose the true meaning. It must not be an excuse for selfishness, self-centredness or independence, whereby the term is used against or at Godly leaders or other individuals to get your own way or justify your behaviour.

Spiritual abuse is the wrong handling or mistreatment of a person who is in need of some help, or support, leading to a weakening, or undermining of that person's spiritual walk or life. Although spiritual abuse is similar to emotional abuse as the mind and emotions are mutually involved, it affects the spiritual wellbeing of the individual in a significant way.

- It is an ungodly and improper use of power and authority usually in a church context, which creates a climate of conflict corporately and individually.
- It is a use of gifting, anointing or position to control, manipulate or dominate another person. This is violation.
- It is a control of events and particularly people for one's own personal agenda and selfish benefit.
- It is an undermining of spiritual right, integrity and dignity.
- It intimidates, which brings fear and insecurity.
- It is an abuse of authority, authoritarian, legalistic and judgemental.

Spiritual abuse can be divided in three ways:

- Division - Satan wants to divide. Insecure leaders will divide. Hurting and rejected people will divide.

- Invasion - To be invaded in your personal response to God and told you are out of order is a desperate issue. Having your rights taken away when someone uses their spiritual position to control and dominate. Having your feelings and opinions overridden without any regard for your wellbeing. It is a pressure to make you live up to another's spiritual standard by external performance.
- Violation - A deep wounding to the heart and spirit of a person.

People leave church for many reasons and most are valid. Regretfully some leave damaged and hurt and feel rejected by their friends and particularly their leaders. Sometimes it is the leader who is rejected. Circumstances are such that he or she has to go. Some church groups have successfully merged and unity prevails but there are many more divisions, splits and break ups and all that is seen is disunity. Some people feel so rejected they stay at home and unwittingly become isolated. There are more and more people who love God but do not want to be part of the church. They feel church has become the problem and not the answer.

As I said in Chapter 1, there are still too many women who have been rejected because of their gifts and calling. Some women are better leaders than some men. They pray, prophesy, teach and preach with a greater capability but because they are women, they have not been allowed. Women who react not always in a good way out of their disappointment and pain are sometimes called Jezebels when in fact their cry is a cry to be heard.

It has been said 'Power without love is reckless and abusive; power at its best is love implementing the demands of justice.'

Statements such as these may be familiar to those of you who have come under the type of leadership, which would want to impose or intimidate rather than serve.

- "I am the will of God for you because God has set me over you."
- "God has told me, therefore you will obey."
- "You cannot question the leader's decisions or authority."
- "This is the way we do it here."
- "My interpretation of scripture is right."

This speaks of exclusivity and elitism and will lead to spiritual damage. There must be room given for honest communication. Sometimes a person may have a perception of these types of remarks through the attitude, personality or character of a leader who gives the impression of not caring. Leaders are carers by calling and serve with humility. They are also human and get hurt but openheartedness and good communication given with integrity can overcome, which is what the people desire. Often it is not the intention to hurt or wound anyone. Words are spoken out of sincerity and a perception of caring and obedience to God. However, what is interpreted is control and a sense of harshness, as words can tear down rather than build up. The church needs a culture of honour not arrogance and pride that creates fear, guilt and shame.

Spiritual abuse is not just a leadership issue. Anyone can exercise control expressed with manipulation, domination or intimidation. A person does not have to be a bully, or a blustering loud-mouthed individual. You can be a quiet, timid person and still exert a power over people.

Victims of spiritual abuse can be many and varied. No one seems to be immune although more than likely it comes out of a place of power or perceived power. Abuse can be sourced from a religious, legalistic, fundamental, elitist or superior type background. There would be little expression of the Father's heart for 'hurting people, hurt people' and if they are in a position of power it is easier to damage others. The people in the church that are loyal and committed and serve, in spite of whatever is going on seem to be easier to be taken advantage of. The problem with a pressure to conform is that it brings out religious performance and perfectionism with a desire to please leadership and not get it wrong.

Regretfully, certain personality traits we thought we had dealt with rear up again to affect us, such as shame, humiliation and even betrayal. These are all such painful emotions caused by an awareness of guilt or shortcoming in behaviour or position, leading to feelings of being disgraced, censured and dishonoured. The power of rejection will infiltrate, undermining self-image creating a low sense of wellbeing and worth with a feeling of deserving to be punished. Often anger and bitterness will be expressed at the perpetrators, which will affect others and the problem develops.

Spiritual abuse often leads people to question their standing with God. They think that they cannot live up to the expectations demanded of them. They perform out of fear and guilt to try to attain a higher level and as they fail they wonder whether it is time to give up.

It has been said, "One of the greatest ironies of the history of Christianity is that its leaders constantly give in to the temptation of power even though they continue to speak in the name of Jesus, who did not cling to His divine power but emptied Himself."

MEMORY POINTS

- All kinds of abuse can cause rejection.
- Rejected people have an ability to abuse others.
- The roots of rejection can be prevalent in a victim's life.
- Abuse is varied and will affect every area of life.
- Abuse is growing in society and can damage an individual mentally, emotionally, physically and spiritually.
- The core of abuse is an improper and inappropriate use of authority and power.
- Control is a key defining factor.
- Emotional and verbal abuse is sourced in all forms of abuse.
- Emotional abuse often develops as a cycle.
- Abused people can react in a way that would cause damage to them personally.

BE PREPARED

'Only the broken become masters at mending.'

The Samaritans were an abused and rejected people.

The relationship between the Jews and Samaritans was one of hostility, and hatred between them was fierce and longstanding, partly due to a division when the Samaritans refused to accept Jerusalem as their holy place and claimed Mount Gerizim as their place to worship God. They also intermarried with people from other tribes after returning home from the captivity (2 Kings 17:24). Jewish and Samaritan leaders taught it was wrong to have any contact with each other and that neither group was to enter each other's territories or even speak to one another. That is why the Samaritan woman said to Jesus, *"how is it that you, being a Jew, ask me for a drink since I am a Samaritan woman? For Jews do not associate or have dealings with Samaritans"* (John 4:9). This is a powerful story because Jesus broke through the barriers of a major conflict showing care, compassion and concern to the woman as well as revealing her heart.

Jesus told a parable, which illustrated loving God and your neighbour, and used a Samaritan as the key person in the story (Luke 10:25-37). The neighbour was someone who showed the love of God to all who were in need whoever they were.

Jesus answered the question, "who is my neighbour" by telling the people to follow the Samaritans example, "go and do the same." We see a Samaritan man, rejected and hated by his neighbours, moving in compassion and love, giving generously and freely, without expectation of return, bringing healing and comfort to one of those neighbours. Portraying a Samaritan in a positive light would have come as a huge shock to Jesus' audience.

We have a mandate to bring healing to the hurting, even to the point where the rejected can bring the love of God to other rejected people. No matter how broken we have been, we can help others feel accepted, valued and restored in society.

PERSONAL HISTORY QUESTIONS

In the counselling or ministry procedure, I have found it very helpful to ask a series of questions relating to the history of the client. Not only does it save time using this method, but it can also pinpoint specific issues, which can then be followed up. I have often given the questions at the beginning of the time together and asked the client to get back to me after a week or so which, gives them time to answer honestly and clearly.

These questions will open up a person to the issues in their life and family that could be important in their healing. Asking the right question, is of course, vital and as they are looked at we need to trust the Holy Spirit to highlight the right ones. They are not in any specific order and the object will be to get the person to open up as much as possible from conception to the present time.

The questions can be found in Appendix 2.

Planning Prayer and Understanding The Issues

Before prayer it is important to consider some things that should make the prayer for healing and or deliverance less difficult. There should be clarity with regard to understanding the areas that need prayer, i.e. the relevant roots or fruits. Then an understanding with regard to the ways in which we pray, i.e. how to confront any demonic power oppressing the person, or how to release the Holy Spirit in hurt emotions or memories. There may well be a need to prepare for the time of ministry by fasting, prayer or reading specific scriptures.

Responsibility

This can be defined as the person recognising that they have a part to play in healing and wholeness, and being prepared to do something about it. They need to be clear they understand as well as are answerable for their own conduct, behaviour, feelings and actions. Personal accountability for some Christians seems to be rare. It is necessary to take responsibility with regard to rejection. Their behaviour is their behaviour and is in their realm of power and control, not anyone else's. It has been said, 'when you blame others, you give up your power to change.' As they see this and own it, the process of healing will come easier. This will start to build or rebuild self-esteem for, 'the willingness to accept responsibility for one's own life is the source from which self-respect springs'.

One of the big reasons for people not taking responsibility for their lives is low self-esteem. The fact that someone else is probably responsible for much of the bad things that happened may be true, but blame will lead to a victim mentality being created and empowered, that will feed rejection. This can damage relationships, ambitions and achievements. The hurt will not stop until a person comes to a place where they take responsibility for their own life. Not taking responsibility may be less demanding and less painful. It is easier to blame someone else but there is always a price to pay. If responsibility is not taken personal power is given away. Taking responsibility means not trying to escape anymore. Instead it is taking control and face what is going on so that the world and new options open up. It is consistency that really pays dividends and can help achieve so much more.

As self-esteem is built to higher levels you that many smaller problems experienced regularly such as negative thinking, self-defeating behaviour and troubled relationships start to correct themselves. An inner stability will be gained and positive feelings will be achievable without the help of confirmation or support from other people.

Rejection will drive a person to make excuses or try to blame other people or other factors. By taking responsibility he or she are giving yourselves power to shape the outcome and are taking an active and not a passive role in it. Making excuses will prevent him or her from succeeding. A responsible person makes mistakes, but when they do, they take responsibility and make it right. They are responsible for their thoughts and behaviour, whether deliberate or unintentional.

A man or a woman may think that to punish themselves is the same as taking responsibility. There is a massive difference between being personally responsible, which brings empowerment and self-blame and punishment. Blame becomes the way to discharge pain and discomfort whether it is personal or to other people. Rejection will keep a person in this cycle, but they can break out and begin to see great change as they take responsibility.

Making Right Choices – The Will

Responsibility and the will go hand in hand and as this is understood, a person can exercise their will to make the right choice. Before any prayer for healing and sometimes deliverance it is crucial to understand that the need to align the will with God's purposes. It is a personal choice and understanding that is the way forward in the journey to freedom. The man or woman has the ability and the power to choose and are not compelled to determine their course of action.

In the strength of His affection for the Father, Jesus posed a question in the Garden of Gethsemane just before His death. He asked His Father if there was another way. He was overwhelmed by anguish, but before an answer came, He aligned Himself with His Fathers will and went to the cross (Mark 14:35-36). To subject Himself willingly to His Fathers will is inestimable. This is humanity in its fullness as Jesus surrendered to the Father's will. When a person submits their will to the will of the Father they submit to His mercy and grace. Even in sacrifice there is provision.

There has to be balance between the head and the heart. Will you be so ruled by your heart that all logic goes out the window or will you be so ruled by the facts that any sensitivity and internal instinct is lost?

This is a time to take hold of what God has promised and go forward. God set before Joshua and the Children of Israel a challenge to choose as they went forward into the Promised Land. Go forward into your land of God's promises and choose life (Deuteronomy 30:19). The alternative was, for the Children of Israel, death, and to many people the power of rejection has been a living death. Three times God spoke to Joshua to be strong and courageous and not to be afraid or dismayed as they were on the boundary of the Promised Land (Joshua 1:6-9). God was saying be bold and confident for He was challenging fear, which is the opposite of courage.

Fear is a powerful emotion that can dictate behaviour. Do you avoid whatever frightens you? Avoidance means you will not be able to fully pursue your dreams and there is always a measure of fear involved in that. Fear can expose a low level of self-confidence or incite a high level of self-criticism. It is time to confront those fears. There are so many 'fear nots' in the bible, probably enough for one for every day of the year. The reason to resist fear is God himself. He does have plans for you, plans to prosper you and not to harm you, plans to give you hope and a future (Jeremiah 29:11-14). These plans will release you from captivity to fulfilment. The promise from God is, *"do not be afraid, I will help you"* (Isaiah 41:14 NIV). He is reassuring you as you make a decision, the right decision.

It is not only the Father's purpose to give you the Kingdom, it is His good pleasure to give, because of His grace and favour on you (Luke 12:32). In this great promise lies the basis of your confidence, value and esteem. You can then replace discouragement with courage, as you make the right decision and move towards healing.

FORGIVENESS

It is vital to look at forgiveness and unforgiveness in the context of rejection. It is impossible to live in this world without being hurt or rejected. There will probably be someone you hold in unforgiveness. This could include yourself or God.

Eva Kor is a survivor of Auschwitz and medical experiments performed by Dr Josef Mengele (The Saturday Times, 25 April 2015, Opinion). Her twin sister died 22 years ago, her body never recovered from the medical experiments. Not long after her sister's death, Eva discovered something so important that it changed her life. She was the only one who had the power to act on this. Nobody could give her this power and no one could take it away. The revelation was that she could bring healing to herself through the power of forgiveness. She said, "Forgiveness is an act of self-healing, self-liberation and self-empowerment." Forgiving Mengele immediately made her feel she was no longer a victim of Auschwitz or a prisoner of her tragic past and amazingly she felt she was free of Mengele." She continued by saying, "Forgiveness is the best revenge against the perpetrator; everyone can afford it, it is free." Today she refuses to be a victim and considers society is bent on nurturing victimhood for in her opinion the world is full of victims because nobody is making the right effort to help people heal. Eva Kor is passionate about forgiveness. She forgave the Nazis, not because they deserve it but because she deserved it!

Forgiveness is:
- Giving up my right to hurt you for hurting me.
- Wiping the slate clean, cancelling the debt.
- A conscious, deliberate decision to release feelings of resentment or vengeance toward a person or group who have harmed you, regardless of whether you think they actually deserve your forgiveness.
- Letting go of the need for revenge and releasing negative thoughts of bitterness and resentment.
- It is a gift we give to ourselves.
- Forgiveness is to set a prisoner free and discover that prisoner is you.

It is so good to know that the memories of the past can be transformed to a hope for the future. This means you do not have to live with unforgiveness, which locks you into the pain of the past.

Jesus explained this vital issue when Peter came to Him asking a question about forgiveness (Matthew 18:21-35). In his question Peter took it for granted that he must forgive but did not know how often, so he suggested forgiving a person seven times through his life. He did this because the Jews never forgave more than three times (Amos1:6). Jesus responded very clearly much to Peter's surprise, "not seven times but seventy times seven!" Peter's supposed generosity was soundly destroyed. Four hundred and ninety times!

This sounds crazy but it means unlimited, perpetual, unending forgiveness. It is said, "Forgiveness is not an occasional act, it is a constant attitude" meaning that we aim to live in the attitude of forgiveness daily.

Jesus then told a story that clearly explained unforgiveness. The servant who was forgiven so much could not forgive at all! We all think forgiveness is a lovely idea, until we have someone to forgive.

How Forgiveness Affects Us

We have been forgiven much. It far exceeds any amount we might have to forgive. We have been forgiven a debt that we could never repay, which is far, far in excess of anything that we would ever have to forgive. It is not to do with the person deserving to be forgiven but is more an act of love, mercy and grace from the person who forgives. In the story, the master's grace and mercy is motivated by forgiveness and his anger motivated by the unforgiveness of the servant. How does that apply to God and us, with regard to any unforgiveness we might have? Unforgiveness is sin no matter what has happened to you. The issue is not who is right or wrong but forgiveness. Therefore God will judge unforgiveness. Unforgiveness also imprisons the one who cannot forgive. They are held captive in unforgiveness and anger, which can turn into bitterness and resentment. Those in prison will be subject to torture and torment. It is certainly torture having hateful thoughts going around in your head continually. Unforgiveness can be a great barrier in our relationship with God as well as each other.

Forgiveness is a choice but it is also a process. You may have to keep forgiving until the pain goes. We need to forgive the unforgivable because God has forgiven the unforgivable in us. The process can take a long time.

If someone has hurt you, it can:
- Affect the way you see them. Forgiveness will begin to change this.
- Affect the way you feel about them. Forgiveness will begin to neutralise the strong feelings you have. How can you say you are right with God but not with each other? As you forgive and receive forgiveness, God will begin to change your heart towards that person.

- Affect the way you talk about them and to them.
- Affect your basic attitude and rights. Forgiveness will negate the need to get even. We have no rights as Christian people. We need to surrender the right to have a right!
- Affect your ongoing relationship and hinder any new beginning.

Forgiveness is so important in the area of healing and deliverance. God had no obligation to forgive us but he did. We need to get to the place where we can forgive others.

Who are you helping most when you forgive the person who hurt you? You are helping yourself more than the other person. It is easy to think that it is so unfair that you have to forgive, when you have been hurt. They are forgiven but you still have your pain! It does not work like that. When you forgive you give freedom but you also come into a freedom yourself. The scriptural mandate is clear, *"Get rid of all bitterness, rage, anger, harsh words and slander as well as all types of evil behaviour. Instead, be kind to each other tender-hearted, forgiving one another, just as God through Christ has forgiven you"* (Ephesians 4:31-32 NLT).

WHAT FORGIVENESS IS NOT...

Forgiveness is not trying to forget, pretending it did not happen, glossing over or denying the seriousness of the offence. It is possible to remember without holding the pain.

Forgiveness is not condoning or excusing. We excuse a person who is not to blame. We forgive because a wrong was committed.

Forgiveness is not giving permission to continue hurtful behaviours.

Forgiveness is not reconciliation. We have to make a separate decision about whether to reconcile with the person we are forgiving.

Forgiveness brings peace of mind as you free the person from your own corrosive anger and let go of the deeply held negative feelings. You then become empowered to recognize the pain you suffered without allowing that pain to define or control you, enabling you to heal, be healed, and move on with your life.

Rejected people can make a new start and forgiveness gives you that capacity. As you draw on the grace of God you can release that grace to others.

REPENTANCE AND CONFESSION

It is important that repentance is clearly understood in the context of rejection. It is more than a quick prayer; we often make it too cheap. Repentance is a costly issue. It is recognising that our sin is offensive to God and that something needs to be done. There has to be a change of mind, which leads to a change of action. As we change our minds, we can then place our faith in the grace of God *"Repent! Turn away from your offences; then sin will not be your downfall"* (Ezekiel 18:30 NIV). It is a deliberate turning away from the sin and a clear turning into God with a change of lifestyle. *"The time has come,"* Jesus said, *"the kingdom of God is near. Repent and believe the good news."*

- Is repentance necessary? Yes, rejection leads us to sin against ourselves, others and the one who created us. Often our wrong reaction to others, which comes out of rejection, is not necessarily seen as sin, we need to think again.
- A clear example of repentance is the way David responded to God after his sin was exposed (Psalms 51). David reacted clearly and cleanly to the word of God. He could have been so tormented by unforgiveness but when he saw that he was the problem, he took responsibility, responded to God and God met him.

There is pain in repentance (2 Corinthians 7:10). It is called Godly sorrow and is only mentioned this one time in scripture. It relates to grief and the acute sense of sadness experienced as a result of sins committed. This is not self-pity, but a deep regret that brings a change of heart, which can take time.

It is significant to look at what happened when Peter spoke to the crowd about repentance on the day of Pentecost (Acts 2:37-41). *'When the people heard this, they were cut to the heart, and said to Peter and the other Apostles, "Brothers, what shall we do?" Peter said, "Repent!"'* The word penetrated deep into their hearts and they responded with a cry for help. Peter's answer was the way forward. You need to be open to God's word in the same way. It is then that repentance becomes effective.

Repentance and confession are closely linked. As you make the decision to change your mind and respond to the grace of God, it is important to acknowledge and admit your sin to Him. Confession means you are being honest; you realise you have something to confess and acknowledge. It is a heart transaction and when we confess, we declare, we assert, we fully acknowledge in all honesty, that something is so, without doubt or ambiguity. To confess your sins to God is not to tell Him anything He does not already know. Until you confess them, however, they are the gulf between you. When you confess them they become the bridge because you are coming into agreement with Him.

DISAPPOINTMENT

We need to understand that disappointment hinders healing. Many rejected people live in deferred hope, which makes the heart sick (Proverbs 13:12). There has been failure to fulfil the deep longing for affection and acceptance. The years may have stolen much in terms of desire for personal fulfilment and value. This produces a wound of rejection. Out of this frustration and hurt the enemy will look for a foothold as relationships suffer. Hope deferred becomes lost hope and then no hope, and further effort becomes futile. Many people only know the first part of this scripture but the second part is a key, 'a longing fulfilled is a tree of life'. Acknowledge the pain of disappointment and make a choice to move away from disappointment and connect with the best part of the scripture. Hope not only means things will get better, it also means we can make things better. God is with us to give us a future and a hope. Remember, *"for a tree there is always hope. Chop it down and it still has a chance - its roots can put out fresh sprouts. Even if its roots are old and gnarled, its stump long dormant, at the first whiff or scent of water it comes to life, buds and grows like a sapling"* (Job 14:7-9 MESSAGE).

SHAME

Shame is a very personal issue and is often deeply hidden. The cause of the shame is something we would rather ignore. It is often connected to personal humiliation, distress and anguish relating to our part in it. Therefore by definition it will not only keep us in rejection, it will imprison us. Shame is not only feeling bad about who you are, it also is a sense of failure in the eyes of someone else. It is how you perceive others see you and how you see yourself. Shame is related to dishonour and feeling unacceptable. People around you may know nothing about you and your past but that may not stop you condemning yourself and beating yourself up.

Shame relates to a loss of trust in yourself - self-disapproval. Shame affects identity with a loss of self-respect leading to feeling inadequate. In your regret and disappointment you will feel unworthy. If you think your actions have led to an irreparable break in relationships you may react to your shame by hiding yourself. Remember how Adam and Eve hid themselves from God (Genesis 3:8-10).

If you have incurred someone's disfavour by your words or actions, be honest; deal with the issue with integrity. It really is all about perception and we need to learn this otherwise rejection will have a field day.

MEMORY POINTS

- Even the despised and rejected Samaritan moved with compassion to help a wounded Jew.
- Family questions can open doors on keys issues related to rejection.
- Being responsible is foreign to some people but it is critical in the path to wholeness.
- Understanding that exercising the will to make right choices is significant in overcoming rejection.
- You can live a lifestyle of forgiveness. It will transform you.
- Understanding the essence of repentance and confession will open doors to personal healing and freedom.
- Do you live in 'hope deferred' or 'fulfilment is a tree of life?' Things can be different because of the grace and mercy of our loving heavenly Father.
- As you understand the significance of personal shame, and the fact that hiding from God is denial you can make a choice to face the shame and *'lift up our eyes to the Lord'* (Psalm 121:1-2) to live continuously in His love and presence.

HEALING PRAYER
- PART 1

"For the sake of His great name the Lord will not reject His people, because the Lord was pleased to make you His own" (1 Samuel 12:22 NIV).

It is important to note that the following two chapters are not a manual of how to do it, giving you specific step-by-step directions. There will be some principles, for example not explaining how to release emotions but understanding why they are vital in the process of healing.

To glean a specific methodology of Jesus' healing is not possible, for there were so many variations and to just concentrate on one will lead to the detriment of another. Jesus used a variety of methods, that show that to always rely on the same procedure is unwise. It is not technique; it is the power of God.

A clear example of this is how Jesus healed eyes. There are many occasions when Jesus healed eyes (Matthew 9:27-31, 20:29-34, Mark 8:22-26, 10:46-52, John 9:1-7) all in different ways, including touching them, deliverance from demons, a release of compassion, declaring the man's faith has healed him and using His saliva. How unusual or even bizarre is this! Jesus spat on the ground made mud with His saliva, formed the mud into two balls and put them on the eye sockets of the man. As the man obeyed Jesus and washed his eyes, he was totally healed. This can be seen to be connected to Genesis, creation and the dust of the earth (Genesis 2:7). It has been said that as DNA is in the saliva the blind man received a divine DNA transfer.

As we see the ways Jesus prayed for the healing of eyes, it seems reasonable to say there is not one specific way to pray for rejected people or in fact anyone. We have to consider the fact that everyone is different and unique and that alone should guide us. There are, of course, principles we need to look at in the specific areas of prayer but we do need the guidance of the Holy Spirit and a sense of discerning before we move forward.

Before prayer ministry it is essential to remind ourselves of the basic biblical groundwork necessary. There are certain imperatives for us to consider to ensure that we move from the right foundation.

- We are in Christ and He is in us and we know we are more than conquerors through Him who loved us (Romans 8:37). In other words we rest in His victory. In that context we can *'possess our possessions or inheritance'* (Obadiah 17). Jesus looked at the individual, the situation and context and then did what His Father showed Him (John 5:19). We pray in the power of the name of Jesus. Jesus said to the disciples, *"these signs will follow those who believe: In my name they will cast out demons, they will lay hands on the sick and they will recover"* (Mark 16:15-17). *"Faith in the name of Jesus, has given complete healing to this man"* (Acts 3:16 NIV).
- Jesus has given us, as He did His disciples, the power and authority over all demons and to cure diseases (Luke 9:1-2).
- We have the Holy Spirit who leads and directs us, bringing revelation where necessary. He has gifted us and, as we respond to Him as the giver, He will give gifts to each of us just as He determines (1 Corinthians 12:11 NIV).
- Understand the place of the cross in prayer ministry. *'He has delivered us from the power of darkness and having disarmed principalities and*

powers, Jesus made a public spectacle of them, triumphing over them in it' (Colossians 1:13-14, 2:15).

All of this is clearly summed up in the following scripture, *'How God anointed Jesus of Nazareth with the Holy Spirit and with power, who went about doing good and healing all who were oppressed by the devil, for God was with Him'* (Acts 10:38).

We have a glorious mentor who went around doing good and healing all. We also have a biblical base. Let us be aware of it and move from it as disciples of Jesus seeing people set free.

WHO IS MY NEIGHBOUR

In the previous chapter we looked at the 'Good Samaritan' as a mandate to bring healing to broken people. In this parable there is more to be aware of as we move into healing (Luke 10:25-37).

Jesus was often challenged and tested by the leaders and exponents of the law, who continually tried to catch Him out and undermine Him. As they discussed a key area, the cornerstone of the Jewish faith, which was to love God and to love your neighbour as yourself (Deuteronomy 6:5, Leviticus 19:34), a lawyer tried to justify his opinion that some people were non-neighbours.

Then Jesus told the story of the Samaritan, which to the people listening, had a clear meaning and challenged them and their culture. The conclusion of the story shows us that the one who showed mercy proved to be the neighbour. It did not matter if the Samaritans were hated and despised by the Jews because this Samaritan was the only one who showed grace and compassion to the wounded man, who in all probability was a Jew.

The answer to us is the same. Whoever we minister to is our neighbour and Jesus, who expounds the law of love, shows us that we can become like the Samaritan and, despite our past rejection, reach out to bring healing to the rejected today. It did not matter that the man was a Samaritan for, unlike the others who did not care, he had compassion and showed it by stopping and caring. It did not matter who the wounded man was because love overcame prejudice and a man's life was saved.

The parable exposed the people who ignored the beaten man and acknowledged the Samaritan who saw a man who needed help. It also serves to give us some guidelines when ministering to a wounded person. The Samaritan came to where the wounded man was and identified with him: he took care of the man and we are called to care of the hurting and wounded, and bring them healing in Jesus name.

This challenging parable gives us keys in helping those damaged because of rejection.

COMPASSION

The Samaritan showed compassion as he saw the state of the man. Compassion is co-suffering, an active desire to alleviate or ease another's suffering. It is more than sympathy and even empathy because of its depth of passion. The word highlights an arousal and expression of love; an identifying in love with mercy, when confronted with those who are sick and vulnerable. Can you imagine the despised Samaritan loving the feared Jew? A rejected man out of a rejected nation overcame the stigma and did something about it. He reached out with kindness. Love is a lifestyle that by the grace of God will enable us to be instrumental in changing lives.

Compassion is identifying with Jesus as He saw the needy people. *'When Jesus saw the multitudes, He was moved with compassion for them, because they were weary and scattered, harassed and helpless, like sheep having no shepherd'* (Matthew 9:36).

Compassion was motivational in Jesus' ministry. There was so much compassion within Him that it poured out of Him in a release of divine power, meeting the needs of the people. Jesus is not cold and unfeeling; He is not distant and reserved but is tender and kind. He is our high priest who was touched with the feelings of our infirmities (Hebrews 4:15 KJV).

WOUNDS – SHOCK AND TRAUMA

The Samaritan bound up the man's wounds. The word 'wound' is only used once in the New Testament and means 'trauma.'

Shock and trauma are very much linked. Trauma is the result of a significant shock and it can create substantial and lasting damage emotionally, mentally as well as physically. So trauma can be the effect or consequence of shock. Shock then can be defined as alarm, fright, or distress coming out of something surprising and upsetting, which is threatening and damaging.

The Samaritan bound the man's wounds. It could be said he bound his trauma. He bound the physical manifestation of the trauma and then began a process of care that certainly helped the man's emotional and mental disturbance.

Part of the ministry of Jesus, which was prophesied and then proclaimed by Him was to *'bind up the broken hearted'* (Luke 4:18). We are called to do the same in His name, because many rejected people still live with the disturbing and troubling consequences of past traumas, however long ago the incident was.

It seems clear that shock and trauma probably affects many more people than we realise, and we can help by bringing the healing of Jesus to them.

POURING

As the Samaritan bound the wounds he poured on oil and wine. He was generous, he gave what he had, which is like the love of God being poured out in our hearts by the Holy Spirit (Romans 5:5). Remember to love your neighbour because as the love of God is poured out in our hearts, we can do the same to others. The word poured is comparable to water gushing out in large quantities to give life and bring healing.

Oil And Wine

Both oil and wine were household remedies used for wounds. Wine was for cleansing, a disinfectant to clean the wound, which relieved pain. The oil coated the wound and enhanced the natural healing process by softening the wound and healing bruises and lacerations. Oil and wine are a symbol of the Holy Spirit who cleanses, comforts, soothes, heals and restores joy to broken people. As the Messianic prophecy states, it is the oil of gladness or joy that is given instead of mourning (Isaiah 61:3). Wine too can indicate joy; *'drink your wine with a joyful heart for God favours what you do'* (Ecclesiastes 9:7). Wine at a Jewish wedding was not just culturally important but it was a significant part of the joyful celebration. There was an occasion when Jesus miraculously provided an abundance of wine, which was heralded as the best (John 2:1-11). Jesus brought transformation by providing the best wine at the wedding.

Continuing Care

In no way would the Samaritan leave the man by the side of the road after he had finished binding his wounds. He put him on his own donkey and took him to an inn, a place of comfort and sustenance. He took care of him and in his kindness and generosity the Samaritan actually gave money to the landlord to look after him for a number of days. The Samaritan put the life of the beaten man before his own because it was dangerous for a Samaritan to be in that situation. Things could get out of hand in view of the Jewish hatred of his people, but he did it and this was the lesson in the parable. He became the Jewish man's neighbour and put his life on the line, in the exercise of love and care.

Past experience says that ministering to rejected people does need consistency, and that leaving them in some healed state 'by the side of the road' will only feed the very rejection we want healed. Aftercare is as important as initial ministry and we need to create a context where the rejected person will not be left without some form of consistent care.

MEMORY POINTS

- This is not a point-by-point manual to be used to heal rejection.
- Look at the diversity of Jesus in healing, such as His healing of eyes.
- Understand the necessity of moving from a basic biblical foundation as you begin prayer ministry.
- Who is you neighbour?
- Follow the steps the Samaritan made in giving help to the damaged Jew.
- Continuing care is very important.
- The Samaritan showed such a commitment to the wounded Jew, his 'enemy' through compassion and love.

HEALING PRAYER
- PART 2

As consideration is given to the following areas, remember this is not a definitive guide. There are already many books written on this, but experience gained over the years has given some further understanding. The idea is to encourage you to think, discern and rely utterly on the Holy Spirit. Bear in mind that these subjects although dealt with in isolation can overlap and connect with each other.

DEMONS

- I have known people who have been damaged in prayer ministry when an expression of emotional pain has been seen as demonic.
- Understand the difference between the emotions and the demonic. The demonic feed on the emotions and the emotions feed the demonic. Remember they are separate entities; it is necessary to separate the demonic from the emotions in Jesus name and deal with them accordingly.
- What about demonic manifestation? We need care as to how we handle it. Do not base your judgements on the manifestation but rely on the Holy Spirit for discernment.
- It is unwise to have conversations with demons; it is unhealthy. As

it is such an emotionally charged time this can become deceptive and manipulative. Years ago a friend and I discerned a lying spirit during a ministry time. As I commanded the spirit to leave, it said "I'm not here!" As humorous as it is, it does make a point. Jesus once asked the name of a demon (Mark 5:9). The answer was "Legion for we are many," probably 6000. This was certainly the exception. Do we think Jesus did not know? Of course He knew but maybe He wanted us to know the power of the demonic and the state of the person.

•   We need to get used to phrases like 'I come in the authority of Jesus' and 'I command you in Jesus name' when casting demons out. This is not a time to be timid or fearful. Speak to the specific and cast them out praying in Jesus' name. It is wise to keep your eyes open so that you are aware of the situation.

•   At the end of ministry encourage the person to take their stand in the freedom that Christ has made for us and not to be entangled again with the oppression of the enemy (Galatians 5:1). Set in place, if possible, follow up and further care.

GENERATIONAL POWERS

In principle generational or ancestral powers, that are connected to the source of rejection can be dealt with by appropriating and declaring the power of the cross, blessing the Godly soul ties and breaking ungodly soul ones, between the person and their family, if necessary back to the third and fourth generation, and then dealing with the demonic in Jesus' name. As well as specifically dealing with the generational power of rejection, consideration should be given to the roots; self-rejection, fear of rejection and rebellion and any controlling spirit manipulating the situation.

SOUL TIES

•   We all have free will and the power to choose whom we relate to, but often this has been distorted and abused, and these rights have not been respected.

- Wrong emotional ties and wrong bonding can affect relationships to the point of rejection both by family members and by people who have influenced us over the years.
- This may lead to manipulation, domination, intimidation and control and these areas need to be dealt with separately. It is not difficult in these circumstances to be tied into a fear of rejection, an ungodly self-protection and anger. It is clear that these issues cause deep wounding and can even open doors for the demonic to take ground.
- Recognise and bless the good and Godly soul ties.
- Remember Godly soul ties are developed in a healthy and wholesome way with family or others as a result of decisions and choices.

Emotions And Inner Healing

- Emotional pain is the accumulation of the response in our feelings to the bad things that have happened, mainly circumstantially or relationally, which create a spontaneous sense of disturbance or agitation such as sorrow, fear or anger. Feelings can of course, also be positive such as happiness, excitement or contentment. Emotions exert a powerful force in how we think and behave.
- If since childhood a person has learned to express emotions in a negative way because of rejection, they would probably handle their emotions in an unhealthy way, which would show themselves in an inappropriate emotional response in a situation. This could be either to close the emotions off totally, which results in a person being perceived as unfeeling in a painful situation, or an obvious, perhaps embarrassing overreaction.
- We need not be afraid of unhealed emotions but learn to express them appropriately with reality.
- God has a deep interest in our emotions and wants to be involved in healing any wounds and seeing them expressed in a right way.
- In fact God is so concerned about our emotions, He has a bottle to collect our tears and a book to record them (Psalm 56:8). The

culture at the time related to the custom of collecting tears shed in a time of sorrow, and either preserving them as a memorial to grief, or placing them in the grave at the funeral as a symbol of respect. God is so committed to us personally that He knows our every affliction and collects every tear shed and records every circumstance with a tender concern. This is a divine expression of care for us to keep our pain and distress stored in His memory, and to bring us relief.

- At the appropriate time in ministry invite God to come, by the Holy Spirit, into the damaged area to release the pain. He understands the depth of our pain. We walk by faith and we trust God's timing.

- It is probable that at this time there will be what is known as a 'catharsis.' This can be described as a genuine deep release of pain, which will purify, purge, and cleanse in the healing process. Having to relive any painful experience of the past is not what is being said, but a release of past pain that is still trapped.

- When Joseph was reconciled to his brothers, *'he wept so loudly that the Egyptians and Pharaoh's household heard him'* (Genesis 45:2). However this does not always happen and we have seen healing when someone has felt deep peace and a sense of lightness or something else of significance to him or her. Nothing is predictable.

- Pray for a revelation of the Father's love and healing to the wounded emotions.

HEALING THE ADULT AND THE HURT CHILD

I have met many adults who were rejected and damaged in various ways in the early years of their lives. Sometimes the pressure had been so great the only way to cope and basically survive was to deny the pain and forget the problem. When a person is faced with something that is too uncomfortable to accept, it is easier to be in denial and insistence that all is fine despite what may be overwhelming evidence to the contrary. Children are so apt at doing this because it becomes their only way of survival. The problem is that these issues do not go away, they just get hidden, but sometime in the future these events, problems and traumas will come back and haunt.

The escape mechanism becomes a survival technique. A child learns they cannot run physically from a trauma, so they separate or dissociate themselves from the situation by escaping to a safe place inside themselves. We all have an ability to deny, or in other words, push the problem away from our consciousness.

The problem is buried as far away as possible. Think of the iceberg, which we looked at earlier, simply defined as conscious (surface), sub-conscious (just below the surface) and unconscious (depth). The involuntary reaction is to push the trauma away as far as possible. It does not disappear it becomes a 'frozen' memory.

FROZEN MEMORIES

Please be aware that there may be some words mentioned here that could be unusual. These are words that I am now used to in view of my experience and personal testimony. I have found that they fit well into a challenging subject. For example, the expression 'frozen memory' simply defines the procedure that happens if we cannot cope with a traumatic experience; the memory is frozen. Remember the word trauma is only used once in the New Testament in the parable of the Good Samaritan (Luke 10:34) and means 'wound or injury.'

We have all been in situations where we shut off or close our minds to what is going on around us through boredom, disinterest or tiredness. It is often called daydreaming. There is a disengaging from reality. At these times it is very difficult to stay focused so there is a tendency to drift.

In a situation of rejection when the pain of a trauma reaches a certain level, the same principle of detaching or disengaging happens. This is a coping or defence mechanism, in which the existence of difficult internal or external realities are kept out of an everyday conscious awareness by denial, and relegation into the sub-conscious. There is a refusal to acknowledge thoughts, feelings, desires, impulses, facts, and events that are unbearable. It seems there is no alternative but to separate or break. None of this is consciously deliberate; it is involuntary and automatic. This allows adults or children to cope and survive traumatic experiences when they would otherwise be affected by degrees of mental and emotional instability. It could be seen as a God given self-protection from mental, emotional and physical pain.

Many people have memories they cannot cope with. Because they cannot cope, they try to forget, and in doing so the memories are locked in time and become frozen memories. These memories do not go away, they remain alive and frozen.

Traumatic experiences can happen at any time. It is an inescapable part of life and at some point some form of trauma will affect every individual. It is possible that trauma will separate the memory of the experience together with the emotion connected to it, and isolate it in the subconscious where it is accessible but avoidable.

It needs to be underlined, everyone is different, and what may be traumatic to one individual may not be traumatic to another. It is the internal understanding of what is a threat, which determines the level of reaction.

Another concept, which overlaps to an extent with the term frozen memory is 'Dissociation.' This can be defined as a separation, a detachment or in certain cases a breaking.

In prayer ministry it is important that there is clarity relating to dissociation. Experience tells us that there are degrees of dissociation connected to the type of trauma experienced by people. It is probable that frozen memory can affect anyone but only a few would experience dissociation, leading to a personality being broken as a result of severe trauma. We need to be aware that there is a difference between separation and brokenness. It is clear that a frozen memory brings separation but it does not always lead to brokenness.

It was 1971 and I remember so clearly when Chris was diagnosed with MS. One morning she went to the doctors to check out some numbness in her left hand. I was in my office in the centre of Bristol and the phone rang. It was the doctor who in no uncertain terms told me my wife was very ill and that I needed to come home immediately as she was getting a consultant to come to the house to examine Chris. I thought she was dying. I rushed home, got to the drive of our house and saw the doctor waiting for me by the front door. As I got out of the car she said words I did not understand, 'multiple sclerosis'. I had no idea what she was talking about. As she said this I heard Chris scream because she knew of someone who had MS and had died. In the shock and trauma of that moment 'I froze'. I was not aware of doing that but it happened. I never forgot that moment but the memory and the pain connected to it were locked away.

In 2007 I was on a speaking tour in Canada and involved in some conferences. One free evening at a friend's house I had some prayer ministry and through that I realised that the memory I had of Chris' diagnosis was frozen. At the moment I heard those words from the doctor, the shock and trauma caused my nervous system to shut down and the memory became frozen. We did have a difficult time in those early years because I had problems accepting the reality of Chris' illness. In that time of prayer I had a very clear vision and in part of it I knew I had to get through a door I was facing to receive something from the Lord concerning my destiny. However the door would not open; it seemed there was a blockage. I turned to look at the wall on my right side and I saw a picture of me getting out of the car with the doctor in the doorway of our house. It was exactly as I have just described. It was the frozen memory of the scene from all of those years ago. I shared it with the others and it was clear the Lord wanted me to embrace the memory. As I did this the door opened. When I returned home I told Chris about my experience. Three months later she said to me, "you have really changed in your attitude to my illness." She had recognised over those few months that I was different.

The very day after the prayer time at my friend's house I was speaking in a ministry centre just north of Toronto, Canada. I was talking about what had happened to me the night before related to frozen memories and the way we deny and suppress issues we cannot cope with. As I was coming to a close and asking the Holy Spirit to do a deep work in lives, a lady who was a lawyer came to the front and asked to share something. It was one of those divine moments. She said she had just had an encounter with Jesus. As I was praying she saw Jesus walk towards her and look into her at the hurt and damaged little girl who was behind bars. He pulled the bars apart, and embraced the child and brought healing to her. The little girl was locked into a frozen memory related to severe abuse. Although she had some memory, in order to survive the trauma she dissociated and held the pain for many years until Jesus came at that moment. As Jesus held her she was integrated into the adult and wholeness came.

SUMMARY

You can see two very different situations that have some connection.

First of all there is no doubt the shock and trauma I felt when I heard about Chris' illness caused a shutting down within me and the pain and the memory were separated from conscious reality. The memory became frozen and I experienced, those many years later, a release and healing. I was able to move on into more of my destiny as I embraced that hidden memory.

The woman who dramatically responded had been severely abused as a child and in order to survive her personality broke. She dissociated and the little girl behind bars was locked in time. The frozen memory was there but the extreme trauma led to a breaking of her personality. This was a sudden, divine intervention as Jesus came and brought healing with integration of the little girl into the adult.

GET IN TOUCH

It is clear there is a need to get in touch with frozen memories in order to bring release and healing. We need to be honest and take responsibility because they are our memories. Here are some principles, which we found have helped many people:

- Jesus is the same, yesterday, today and forever (Hebrews 13:8).
- Jesus transcends time so we can ask him to go back, however far in time, to the event and heal yesterday's problems today. It is so easy for Him.
- Repent of unforgiveness and denial.
- Bind and separate any demonic torment and oppression in Jesus' name from any connection or influence it has on the memory.
- Command the spirits of shock and/or trauma to leave in Jesus' name. There may be other demonic oppression such as rejection, infirmity and death connected to this, which may need to be told to leave.
- Face, accept and embrace the painful memory.
- Invite the Holy Spirit to come and divinely integrate the memory.
- There may well be a catharsis, a release of the pain.
- Speak peace. *"And the peace of God, which surpasses all understanding, will guard our hearts and minds through Christ Jesus"* (Philippians 4:7).
- There will be Shalom, wholeness.

The scriptural context here relates to the term broken hearted:

- The Lord is close to the broken hearted (Psalm 34:18 NIV). He is close enough to touch.
- He heals the broken hearted and binds up their wounds (Psalm 147:3).
- Jesus heals the broken hearted (Isaiah 61:1, Luke 4:18).

Broken things in this world are usually rejected as worthless and thrown away.

Sometimes the trauma is powerful enough to shatter a life.

INTEGRATION

The idea of coming to terms with the past through healing frozen memories and dissociation can be summed up in the word 'integration.' Integration is a joining, assimilation or absorption of the separated frozen memories and any broken part of the personality.

As traumatic experiences and frozen memories that have been separated are reprocessed and unlocked through prayer ministry, integration will take place as the memories are accepted and embraced.

In dissociation it is important that integration is seen as a joining of the broken personality into the whole. The woman mentioned earlier who was abused and broken and the traumatised, damaged little girl who was still behind bars after all of these years met Jesus. He came to her; embraced her and integration came, as the woman was made whole.

The intention is to achieve resolution so that the healed person can move into their destiny in God with no further blockages or hindrances.

THE WOUNDED SPIRIT

The human spirit is an amalgam of intuition, knowledge of God, conscience, which discerns truth and judges between right and wrong and also communion and communication with God. It is the place of relationship with God.

When the spirit is wounded, it is as though the very source of our life in God is affected, for as Jesus said, *"the words I have spoken to you are spirit and they are life"* (John 6:63). We know the spirit can be damaged, *'a man's spirit sustains him in infirmity or sickness but a wounded or crushed spirit who can bear'* (Proverbs 18:14 NIV).

As I wrote earlier: *"For there is hope for a tree, if it is cut down, that it will sprout again and that its tender shoots will not cease. Though its root may grow old in the earth and its stump may die in the ground, yet at the scent of water it will bud and bring forth branches like a plant"* (Job 14:7-9).

The wounded spirit is like a damaged tree. The sustaining and nurturing water of the Holy Spirit can be imparted and any damaged part of the spirit can be called to life. Jesus is the resurrection and the life. We have the life to sustain us and release to others in His name (John 11:25). The presence of the Holy Spirit within us calls "Abba Father" (Galatians 4:6) and He wants to draw us closer to Father God to restore the tree.

PRAYING FOR CHILDREN

Obvious sensitivity, wisdom and discernment are important when praying for children. Best practice must come to the forefront here with parents being involved every step of the way. I have made it a habit to pray for children under ten, when they are asleep. That is not to say never involve children in prayer; it may be right to communicate with them but it does depend on the wishes of the parents and the child. They need as much honour and respect as we do. We should not be afraid of praying for children and of course the child in the womb. Being proactive by praying blessing and protection on the child is so important. We need to be sensitive how we pray and the terminology we use.

Children can be affected in the womb. What happened in the womb of Elizabeth when she met Mary who was pregnant with Jesus? (Luke 1:41) It seemed Elizabeth's excitement and joy affected the baby in the womb. The baby leapt in the womb and Elizabeth was filled with the Holy Spirit. It was a supernatural moment, the release of emotion plus the presence of the Holy Spirit. It was an extraordinary occurrence, which affected the baby. Luke had already mentioned that John was filled with the Spirit in his mother's womb. What an amazing experience at the beginning of his life before his birth!

If the child in the womb can be filled with life, joy, the blessing of God and so much more good and positive things, can bad experiences; negative words and even curses also affect him or her? Having prayed with many people who knew they were not wanted before their birth, it is clear that destiny and identity begin in the womb. Many children are born with rejection and behave accordingly, and it will continue to affect them as they grow into adulthood.

Praying to cut off any generational sin or soul ties to the third and fourth generation as soon as possible after the child is born is important. There is nothing like blessing the child as it comes into this world but also releasing it from anything negative, including rejection, is necessary.

'Train up a child in the way he should go, and when he is old he will not depart from it' (Proverbs 22:6). This can be such a positive step but have you ever thought of the reverse? 'Train a child up in rejection and when he is old he will not depart from it.' If that is so, the power of rejection could affect a person all their life unless they are set free from it. Once rejection or any other wrong belief is established in a young life, it is not easy to shift it because as the child grows, the roots will also grow unless the power of God breaks in and brings freedom.

MEMORY POINTS

- This is not a manual but a sharing of some principles learned through experience in ministry and revelation by the Holy Spirit.
- Understand and distinguish between the demonic and emotions.
- Do not let demonic manifestation and demons speak to you to control and deceive you. You have the authority to deal with these things.
- Remember the consequences of both Godly and ungodly soul ties.
- Emotions seriously influence how we think and behave.
- God wants wholeness in our emotions and His concern goes as far as collecting our tears.
- Remember 'catharsis' and the necessity of releasing the pain as a step towards healing.
- Consider 'Frozen Memories' and the fact that traumatic experiences and the way we respond to them have a key part to play in our lives.
- We can get in touch with the frozen memory and know integration and resolution as we embrace it in Jesus' name.
- Dissociation can occur when the personality is broken through severe trauma and there can be integration but remember, in this context, dissociation is not that common.
- Children as well as adults quickly learn how to deny and suppress trauma and pain.
- Honour children by being proactive, blessing them and praying for them. In this we affect their identity and destiny in a positive way.

The King's Table

We saw in Chapter 2 an amazing example of rejection when Mephibosheth lost his identity, his family and his inheritance when he was five years old. He was a Royal Prince and his nurse, afraid that his father and grandfather's enemies would come after him, attempted to hide him and, in the ensuing escape dropped him and he became crippled (2 Samuel 4:4).

He was taken to Lo Debar and left where no one could find him. It was a city characterised by its barrenness and wastelands, a desolate place known as a land of nothing. Mephibosheth was hidden from everyone and he lived like rejected person. It seems he lived in Lo Debar many years, maybe up to fifteen, because he had married and had a son (2 Samuel 9:12).

Through all this time he carried:
- Physical pain - He was crippled, he could not walk and it is probable someone had to carry him wherever he went.
- Mental pain - Besides rejection there was probably depression, fear and among other things, loneliness.
- Emotional pain - He was deeply damaged emotionally and possibly an angry man.

- Spiritual pain - It is obvious that his spirit would have been wounded and damaged.

MEPHIBOSHETH THE HURT CHILD

A child arrives in this world with a deep thirst for relationship. There is a longing for something he or she does not have but needs in order to survive; a relationship where the child is regarded as someone of great value and worth. A child cannot find this within him or herself and will reach out to be content and fulfilled. A baby has no self-awareness but that soon begins to change, and its concept of self will largely depend upon what is mirrored by people who mean the most to them.

Who was the closest to Mephibosheth? Certainly his father Jonathan and grandfather Saul, but there is no mention of his mother. Some speculate she had died and a nurse looked after him. Mephibosheth would have looked to his father and grandfather for love and acceptance and to some extent his nurse. If the child does not get the love it needs, it is likely rejection will begin to develop in his or her life.

What happened to Mephibosheth was that he did receive that love but it was stolen away. The shock and trauma of losing his father and grandfather in battle on the same day, plus becoming crippled because the nurse dropped him, opened doors of intense and severe physical, emotional and mental pain. This led to rejection, abandonment, isolation and desolation.

Children learn very early to lessen or relieve frightening memories by numbing or disconnecting them. Mephibosheth must have felt so frightened and utterly helpless. The people he loved and trusted most had left him alone. The situation that Mephibosheth found himself in happened so suddenly, and he was powerless to prevent it. He was only five years old and an orphan. This is trauma.

Mephibosheth's traumas as a child probably led him to create rigid and inflexible boundaries, a wall of self-protection. In his attempt to survive he would not let anyone near him. He became withdrawn; he must have hated himself and was angry at what he had become. He stayed in his own safe area of unbelief, doubt and fear. Life had treated him very badly but despite that he married and had a child.

THE CALL OF THE KING

David had finally become king over all Israel and, after a while, as things settled in the nation, David remembered his relationship with Jonathan and asked about Saul's family. It was not about revenge or even self-preservation, because the king of a new dynasty had the right to massacre anyone of the old order (2 Samuel 9:1-13). David did not action this right; he had something he wanted to do, which was the beginning of healing for Mephibosheth. Even though Saul made David an enemy, love prevailed. David had a strong relationship and covenant with Saul's son, Jonathan, which he wanted to continue with any one still left in the family. Maybe David had never seen Mephibosheth, but he wanted to love him for Jonathan's sake.

When Grace Is Released Healing Begins To Flow.

The power of healing began for Mephibosheth even before he knew what was going to happen. David had a wonderful relationship with Mephibosheth's father, Jonathan. They made a covenant with each other and Jonathan asked David to always show him unfailing kindness, and never cut off that kindness to his family (1 Samuel 18:3, 20:14-16).

The words David spoke, *"is there anyone left"* are full of meaning; he wanted to make things better. A former servant from Saul's household was called and he informed the king there was someone who was crippled and lived far away in isolation. No doubt David's heart leapt when he heard it was Jonathan's son. In no way did David see this as a threat. He wanted to keep the promise he made to Jonathan.

David called this the kindness of God (2 Samuel 9:3). Kindness here means loving faithfulness, which is sourced in God who is the kindest person in the universe. *'God through His great love for us is rich in mercy'* (Ephesians 2:4). This is His expression of grace. David wanted to show favour even as God shows favour, and this was out of a promise made in love not duty. Grace is favour, grace is free, grace is amazing and grace is getting the good we do not deserve, cannot earn and certainly cannot repay. This is kindness not justice for there are no conditions with grace; it comes out of unconditional love.

Mephibosheth had not done anything to merit the favour or the kindness of David. Remember his name means shame. He seems to have had little or no personal worth.

Mephibosheth was:
- A fugitive; so many rejected people understand this.
- He was crippled in both feet; rejected people are disabled regarding their destiny.
- He did not live in Jerusalem meaning 'possession of peace' but he lived in a place called 'nothing.' Rejected people identify with that.

Steps were taken to bring Mephibosheth to Jerusalem. He knew nothing of the reasons why and would have assumed this could be the end particularly when soldiers appeared and told him they had to take him now to see the king. This was a command and it was to be now.

Mephibosheth was no longer hidden. He had felt safe as long as he was out of the way. This was not true and its deception kept him locked up inside himself rather than knowing the grace of God through David, which would enable him to face up to issues and know healing.

Mephibosheth needed to make a choice so imagine the thoughts going through his mind. "What is happening? Why does he want me? What for?" However when the king calls, you obey. It was a conflict. The important question is, 'will the past still continue to control the future?' He needed to let go of the past, to stop history dominating his future destiny. It was a risk and he had to take a step of faith. He obeyed the command of the king and went with his hurt to David's court.

Who is Lord in our lives? We need to see where we are in this. If Jesus is who we say He is, then we will obey Him, for in His heart is grace and mercy for us, which is the beginning of healing from rejection.

Mephibosheth arrived and bowed down to honour the king saying, "your servant." He did not know that David wanted to adopt him as a son. David said, "do not be afraid." Mephibosheth had been in court as a boy and he knew what went on and he was afraid. Fear is a dreadful emotional state, characterised by the anticipation of pain or distress. It is an expectation of danger, "something horrible and cruel is going to happen to me." This fear was genuine for Mephibosheth and was not just occasional but continual. The most repeated command that Jesus gave was "fear not." It seems that 'fear not' is mentioned in the bible 366 times. David said, *I do not want to hurt, kill or punish you because I have good in my heart for you and I want to lift you up not put you down.*

Then Mephibosheth heard something he could hardly believe. David expressed such kindness to him after all the years of pain and isolation. The king spoke with confidence and clarity determining that nothing would stand in his way in bringing restoration. It was unquestionable and indisputable. It seemed that coming into the presence of the king brought up all the emotion and pain Mephibosheth had carried for years. He glanced up to see if in fact this was King David speaking. He quickly put his face to the ground again and said: *Who am I that you should notice a dead dog like me?* What a response he obviously felt useless, hopeless, totally no good, like a Gentile. Wild dogs were the object of dislike and contempt. It seemed anyone who opposed King David, the king chosen by God, was a dead dog. To oppose him was to oppose God; Goliath would have been called a dead dog. Mephibosheth did not think he could expect anything different. It is not difficult for rejected people to believe a lie concerning themselves. The lie about as to how we see ourselves and how we think God sees us, will greatly restrict us in reaching for our destiny and keep us hidden in our Lo Debars.

THE PROVISION OF THE KING

David gave Mephibosheth an amazing promise.

- *"I will restore to you all the land that belonged to your grandfather."*
- *"You will always eat at my table."*

David sought to extend his grace to Mephibosheth and restore his dignity. Mephibosheth had done nothing to deserve this. All he could do was humbly accept it. He had no claim on David and no case to present. What the king wanted was to restore Mephibosheth to his rightful place of sonship, with honour, and friendship and also give back to him all that was taken from him. Sitting at the king's table meant family for he was treated like one of David's sons. He ate continually at the king's table. This was not a temporary honour it was forever. David gave far more to Mephibosheth than he had lost.

David's acceptance of Mephibosheth still says to rejected people, 'it is possible.'

A MESSAGE TO REJECTED PEOPLE

We need to consider what this means to us. What David did for Mephibosheth, in the kindness of God can also be done for us. God wants to restore to us everything that the enemy has stolen. Jesus said, *"The thief comes only to steal and kill and destroy but I have come that you may have life and have it more abundantly"* (John 10:10). Not only does God want to restore to us all that was stolen from us but also as David did with Mephibosheth, give us back much more.

Mephibosheth had:
- His identity restored - He was given worth, value and esteem as a royal prince.
- His family restored - He ate at David's table like one of the king's sons.
- His inheritance restored - The family lands were given back to him.

OUR PROVISION THROUGH THE FATHER'S LOVE

The heart of the king was grace and mercy, which is so like of the heart of God, for He drew us to Himself through Jesus and called us sons! *'But as many as received Him to them He gave the right to become sons or children of God'* (John 1:12). *'You are no longer a slave but a son and if a son then an heir of God through Christ'* (Galatians 4:7).

What did this mean for Mephibosheth? He ate at the table like a son. He not only received the necessities of life but he felt safe, secure and peaceful. He was not alone because he was in family. He was in a place where he could finally trust and he knew healing. He also knew that sitting at the kings table meant he was treated like a son, the king's son with honour. He may have felt like a slave but in David's eyes he was a son.

WHAT THE TABLE MEANS TO US

We have a place where we are invited to commune and communicate with Him. It is our own place of safety and security in Christ. Servants and slaves do not sit at the table; sons do and we are sons.

It is a table set in the presence of our enemies where our heads are anointed with oil and our cup overflows (Psalm 23:5). The shepherd anoints his sheep with oil for two purposes:

- To repel insects. They afflict the sheep and the ewes will stop giving milk and the lambs will stop growing. It is as though the enemy is kept at bay and the flock are at peace.
- To heal wounds. Most wounds result from living with the flock, so the shepherd regularly inspects his sheep because he does not want today's wound to become tomorrow's infection.

'I shall be anointed with fresh oil' (Psalm 92:10). The dirt and grime of the journey quickly contaminate yesterday's oil, so go to God day by day and ask Him to empower you with His Spirit. A sheep does not understand how the oil works, but it does not have to. It is enough to know that something happens in the presence of the shepherd that happens nowhere else. We can understand and, therefore, eagerly look forward to receive a fresh anointing of His Spirit and presence to enable us to walk day by day with Jesus.

'My cup overflows,' which signifies the release and flow of the life of the Spirit on a daily basis too. See more about the Shepherd, in The Good Shepherd chapter (page 85).

UNCONDITIONAL LOVE

What we see in David's response to Mephibosheth is a result of unconditional love. It is a picture of God's unconditional love for us. *'What marvellous love the Father has extended to us! Just look at it - we're called children of God! That's who we really are'* (1 John 3:1 MESSAGE).

- Unconditional love means someone is loved regardless of his or her actions or beliefs.

- Unconditional love leads to unconditional acceptance.
- Unconditional means no conditions; it is absolute and free.
- The pain of the past is real but the joy and delight of being called a son will outweigh any painful experience or circumstance.
- It is not what you have done or what has been done to you; it is how you respond to the giver of grace.

'God did it for us. Out of sheer generosity He put us in right standing with Himself; a pure gift. He got us out of the mess we're in and restored us to where He always wanted us to be. And He did it by means of Jesus Christ' (Romans 3:24 MESSAGE).

What human effort can achieve favour with God? There is nothing we can do because God's justice and righteousness have already been satisfied. We are guilty but have been freely pardoned through God's grace. 'Freely' is such a glorious emphasis of grace.

'Saving is all His idea, and all His work. All we do is trust Him enough to let Him do it. It's God's gift from start to finish. We don't play the major role. If we did, we'd probably go around bragging that we'd done the whole thing' (Ephesians 2:8-9 MESSAGE).

Mephibosheth finally entered into all the goodness and kindness of David with thankfulness in his heart for he could now live in his destiny. Like Mephibosheth we can enjoy all that our loving Heavenly Father has for us.

MEMORY POINTS

- Mephibosheth's traumas happened unexpectedly, suddenly and he was powerless to do anything about it.
- As a five year old he could not rationalise what was happening to him when he was abandoned.

- Rejection overcame him. In his attempt to survive as he grew up he could not let anyone get close to him and withdrew into isolation.
- Years later change began as the David remembered his covenant with Mephibosheth's father and took steps to restore things.
- As grace and kindness was shown healing was released.
- The call of the king brought a wounded and rejected man to the place of restoration.
- Mephibosheth brought with him his fear, his unbelief and all of his negativity and the king was able to deal with it.
- Everything and more was restored to Mephibosheth.
- He was adopted as a son and sat at the king's table continually.
- God's love is unconditional, uncontainable, unfailing, unquestionable, unequivocal and sometimes uncomfortable.
- Unconditional means we can come to Him just as we are and find acceptance and healing.
- If God's love to us is unconditional, can we not act in the same way to others?

MIND GAMES

"Your beliefs become your thoughts. Your thoughts become your words. Your words become your actions. Your actions become your habits. Your habits become your values. Your values become your destiny." Gandhi

Do we think things we hate to admit we think?

One of the greatest works that God wants to do in our lives is the transformation of our thought life.

It is unrealistic to say that after prayer ministry, rejection will never affect us again. It always will, but the challenge is how to respond to it. It has been said that 'there are no easy answers only good responses' and it is this we need to look at in the context of the mind. We are thankful that we can get help regarding all the hurts and wounds of the past and certainly know healing, but how do we prepare ourselves after any ministry for healing? How we react in future situations of rejection is crucial and looking at the way we think is foundational to that.

Sometimes people think that after prayer everything will be ok. However, it is not a time to lower our defences because as issues arise, we will need to change those old mind-sets that influence us in reaction to rejection. They do not change automatically and we cannot cast them out! Thoughts influence us. How we think affects our feelings and then our behaviour. If we are still in an old pattern of thought and the pressures of life continually affect us negatively, we will feel and behave out of rejection, which will make us think nothing has changed.

If we can change our thought patterns we will feel different and also find that our behaviour changes. An example of this could be that a friend did not notice you in the street and crossed the road. What are your initial thoughts? From the mind-set of rejection they will probably be irrational thoughts such as, "he ignored me, how rude, he must have a problem with me." Then you may feel irritated or even angry. Your body may become tense with shoulders hunched and jaw clenched, and you may feel discomfort or even pain in your stomach. Later you find out the person did not see you, they had to cross the road because they remembered something they had to do and so were focused on that. There never was a problem. However, the damage was done and the enemy comes to whisper condemnation to you. You become angry with yourself, opening the door to self-rejection.

We can change these thought processes with the help of our loving Heavenly Father. Ways of thinking become patterns and habits. Then the more we think in a certain way, the less aware we become of these patterns because they become automatic. It is like driving a car; you start as a 'learner' and it seems so complicated as you begin. Soon it becomes less difficult until the various actions become simple and finally automatic. You find yourself doing these things with no effort at all.

We can look at our patterns of thought and begin to change them; get to the place where we can challenge unhelpful and negative thoughts and learn to replace them with good and positive thinking. In the same way we focus as we learn to drive, we can learn be responsible and choose to focus on changing the way we think. It is important then to take a proactive approach to rebuild the frame of mind from the starting point of acceptance and not rejection. The aim is to be able to overcome any sense of rejection that confronts us and our goal is to shape our mind-set so that the vision becomes a reality. It has been said, "When you change the way you look at things, the things you look at change."

Question: Is what we believe reality?

Many ancient cultures believed the earth was flat. They were convinced but we know that is not true. There was also a belief that the earth was the centre of the universe. As scientists began to prove the earth did in fact orbit around the sun with other planets, men such as Copernicus and Galileo in the 16th and 17th century were persecuted and denounced as heretics by the Church. The earth is the centre of the universe was a belief that the Church held and it was their reality. Sometimes beliefs are not reality!

It is important therefore to understand and consider our belief systems and the behaviour cycles that operate out of them.

BELIEF SYSTEMS

Belief systems are established in our formative years through contact with those closest to us, usually our parents. Beliefs, whether positive or negative, create a framework that enables us to interpret and understand life experiences, which in turn will affect the way we behave day by day. Belief systems can be described as lenses, which filter the way we perceive the world.

As we grow up, we receive messages from the adults around us with whom we have important relationships. The interaction in these relationships teaches us to pay attention to certain things in certain ways. They may be good and true or false and destructive. As children we take in and absorb information, but do not have the adult ability or experience to interpret or evaluate too well. These messages influence and shape the belief system and subsequently our world- view, the way we see things, is established.

For example, if you experienced a dog biting you when you were young, you might now be afraid of dogs. In the light of that experience you perceive that dogs will cause you pain and have to be avoided. Your belief system is, 'be very careful around dogs because they bite.' A barking dog may trigger that belief and also trigger fear that you may get bitten again. In reality most dogs do not bite but because of the way in which you have filtered your experience, you believe they do. Someone who has never been bitten by a dog, been brought up with a dog in the family, and has had pleasant experiences, will have a different belief system, which will give a totally different meaning to a dog barking. There will be no fear or anxiety. Beliefs like this will affect our self-confidence and esteem.

We have already looked at how a person can be emotionally hurt and wounded through past experiences, relationships or ongoing circumstances. This will affect the way we live and the way we react. It is possible to live a life full of hurt and pain but not allow ourselves to have a negative attitude. Yet many of us seem to fall into the negative category.

From the hurts, we allow ourselves to develop ungodly habits, reactions, behaviour, and attitudes, which then affect our world-view. These will form a barrier to the work of the Holy Spirit in our lives. The resulting trauma and distress will also, of course, affect our daily walk with God. Basically, our beliefs either will hold us back creating barriers to progress, or help to project us forward into the truth of our destiny.

BEHAVIOUR PATTERNS OR CYCLES

The following is an analysis of an instantaneous automatic reaction in any situation.

Behaviour Patterns or cycles operate out of Belief Systems. From an internal or external trigger, a pattern of behaviour will recur. There is a sequence that rotates in a cyclic way as one response leads to another.

A behaviour pattern or cycle can be defined in the following way:

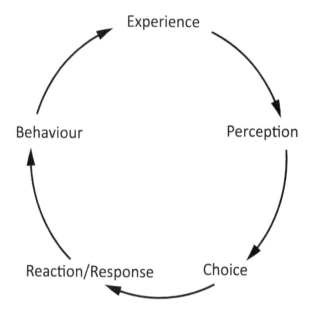

Definition - A cycle is an instant reaction; it is automatic. A man we were counselling explained it like this, 'the button is pressed and the tape runs.'

Experience - An unexpected or challenging encounter with a person or situation triggers the cycle.

Perception - The experience is understood through the lens of perceived truth. Some examples are: "I'm not attractive, so nobody could love me", "I will never trust anybody because I will always be hurt or let down", "I have to please others in order to be liked or valued."

Choice - Because of the lens, which filters incoming information based on the belief system, the choice is automatically made about how to react.

Reaction - This is an emotional reaction defined as 'flight or fight,' aggression or withdrawal or a response in peace out of the security of the Father's love.

Behaviour - Finally, you behave in the only the way you know. So the end result of a behaviour cycle is either rejection and self-rejection or security and acceptance. There are many types of cycles of behaviour. We all relate to the principle but have our own variations.

NEGATIVE BEHAVIOUR CYCLES OR PATTERNS

Here are some examples of specific beliefs and the cycles they may trigger.

Typical Rejection Cycle

Belief: Worthlessness: Lack of nurture and affirmation usually in childhood

Belief: I have no emotional needs: Emotional needs not met in childhood

Belief: I must win to be accepted

You may wonder if cycles are an expression of sin. Sin may certainly be involved, but the cycle may start because you may have been sinned against or because you are justifying your own sin. For example, you may have been rejected at birth and you know that if you perform in a certain way, you will get attention. Maybe once it was the 'supermarket tantrum syndrome;' it is now much more clever. Inner vows too may have been made and the enemy is a legalist, he will keep you to them.

Changing beliefs starts by challenging beliefs. Personal breakthroughs will happen by changing our beliefs. We do not challenge our beliefs because we believe them to be true. It is possible though that what we believe is actually a lie. We need to be aware of any difference between our belief and what God actually says.

CHALLENGE TO CHANGE

Do not cherish negative thoughts. Often we do not realise how much we subconsciously cherish negative thoughts. It may seem counter intuitive, but often a negative mind-set is established because we will not let go of the negative thoughts and ideas. Sometimes the mind clings on to these thoughts because of self-pity or injured pride. We do not like the negativity, but at the same time are we consciously trying to overcome it? The problem is that if we allow the negative thoughts go round and round in our mind, they become powerful and we lose a sense of perspective.

It is important to acknowledge the fact that we all experience negative thoughts. The more you fear them, fight them, or try to avoid them, the stronger their voices will become. As we acknowledge our negative and destructive thoughts, we come into a place where we can begin to deal with them.

Recognition - It is important to identify wrong beliefs and understand their source. This may be the hardest thing of all so try to be honest!
Does the way we were parented influence and affect how we behave? Are our beliefs compatible to scripture?

We certainly need the Holy Spirit alongside, to bring revelation and conviction.

Reflection - This is an owning process. We need to take responsibility. It takes more than a prayer to demolish these belief systems. We also have to do something. Are there people around us that we can share these things with, who we trust to show us a different perspective?

We may need to look at family traits that confirm to us negative beliefs generationally and it is possible that there may be some demonic interference. However bear in mind that this is not a quick deliverance session; it is about taking responsibility for our own problems and being prepared to do something about them.

Repentance - Repentance involves a review, acknowledgement of and taking responsibility for previous actions, with an unconditional surrender to God that includes a commitment to change. In essence, it is a change of mind, a conscious turning away from negative thoughts that are in conflict with our Godly lifestyle. As we challenge these belief systems in the power and love of God in Jesus' name we will begin to change. Consider too, the need to forgive anyone who has controlled to the extent that we made their damaging thoughts our own.

Choice - As we recognise the above points it is crucial that we understand our role in making choices. The negative beliefs and cycles will need to be challenged and broken; in other words we need to take action. We have to take responsibility to make that choice. As we choose to change, we choose to bring all our negative beliefs and cycles to Jesus and make Him Lord over them. The right choice will lead to a right focus. Do not focus on tomorrow, focus on the present, the immediate. When Jesus said, *"I am the resurrection and the life"* (John 11:25). He was focusing on the now not the past or the future. He was declaring what He was and who He is today.

Change In Behaviour - Change will begin as we go through the process. We will have to want to and choose to behave differently. We must learn to affirm our strengths and acknowledge our weaknesses. We may find immediate change but we still have to make choices.

Our perceptions of how God sees us will change and we will begin to send out a different message.

RENEWING THE MIND

In our relationship with God we have a great advantage, because we have the encouragement of Him being our loving Heavenly Father, the authority of Jesus' name and the anointing and power of the Holy Spirit, as well as the revelation of the scripture. Can anything, which seems to sustain the negative beliefs, overcome that force? Surely not, particularly as we determine to break through in the power of Jesus' name.

We can learn to think and live in a renewed way. We do have through the power of the Holy Spirit the passion and ability to change the way we think. Why should we live in the condemnation of rejection daily when we can live fully accepted in the love of the Father.

The following scriptures will help us to align with clear biblical belief:
"I beseech you therefore, brethren, by the mercies of God, that you present your bodies a living sacrifice, holy, acceptable to God, which is your reasonable service. And do not be conformed to this world, but be transformed by the renewing of your mind, that you may prove what is that good and acceptable and perfect will of God" (Romans 12:1-2).

"Be renewed in the spirit of your mind, and that you put on the new man which was created according to God, in true righteousness and holiness" (Ephesians 4:23-24).

"I have been crucified with Christ; it is no longer I who live, but Christ lives in me; and the life which I now live in the flesh I live by faith in the Son of God, who loved me and gave Himself for me" (Galatians 2:20).

"Be anxious for nothing, but in everything by prayer and supplication, with thanksgiving, let your requests be made known to God; and the peace of God, which surpasses all understanding, will guard your hearts and minds through Christ Jesus" (Philippians 4:6-7).

"Your old life is dead. Your new life, which is your real life—even though invisible to spectators - is with Christ in God. He is your life" (Colossians 3:3 MESSAGE).

"Summing it all up, friends, I'd say you'll do best by filling your minds and meditating on things true, noble, reputable, authentic, compelling, gracious - the best, not the worst; the beautiful, not the ugly; things to praise, not things to curse. Put into practice what you learned from me, what you heard and saw and realized. Do that, and God, who makes everything work together, will work you into his most excellent harmonies" (Philippians 4:8-9 MESSAGE).

WEAPONS OF WARFARE

The following scripture is foundational in challenging our beliefs and seeing them change: *"For the weapons of our warfare are not carnal but mighty in God for pulling down strongholds, casting down arguments and every high thing that exalts itself against the knowledge of God, bringing every thought into captivity to the obedience of Christ"* (2 Corinthians 10:4-5).

Consider the inspiring way The Message translates this verse: *"We use our powerful God-tools for smashing warped philosophies, tearing down barriers erected against the truth of God, fitting every loose thought and emotion and impulse into the structure of life shaped by Christ. Our tools are ready at hand for clearing the ground of every obstruction and building lives of obedience into maturity."*

This is such a vital scripture because it shows us clearly our responsibility and our authority in God to bring about change in our lives. We need the affirmation of scripture and learn to declare it in the process of change.

Paul is saying these weapons are not human weapons that rely on human resources such as the power of argument, the manipulation of the human nature or even specific military weapons but they are spiritual. We can move in the Spirit and not the carnality of the flesh. We move with and in the authority of Jesus with the power of the word of truth, praying in the Spirit and ministering the gifts of the Holy Spirit. We are at war but in the victory that Jesus attained we can take ground in our lives. Our purpose is to resist, displace and then fortify ourselves. One of our primary weapons for offence and defence is the sword of the Spirit, which is the word of God (Ephesians 6:17). Jesus said that as we continue or abide in His word we would know the truth and the truth would set us free (John 8:31-32).

MIGHTY IN GOD

We can be strong in the Lord and in His mighty power (Ephesians 6:10). It literally means powerful and effectual for God.

Strongholds - The original word is only mentioned in the New Testament. The meaning literally is a coastal rock fort, a dungeon or fortress and these places are resolutely defended.

In this context the stronghold is a thought or belief pattern that controls and holds you in its grip. It is based on lies and deception and will oppose the truth of who we are in God. Strongholds are birthed in deception. Strongholds cause us to think in ways that keep us from God's best.

The most important strongholds are mistaken and untrue images in our mind of who God is and how He sees us, and also the negative way we think about ourselves. We can start by surrendering to God in these areas.

PULLING DOWN, CAST DOWN

Strong action is necessary to overcome the opposition to the truth of God in our minds. This not only includes anything that sets itself up against the knowledge of God, such as philosophies but also the thought processes and belief patterns of the mind, that would challenge us in our walk with God.

TAKING CAPTIVE EVERY THOUGHT

Once we get this far we will need to remain alert to the ways in which the enemy will try to remind us of our old beliefs and undermine our relationship with God. Satan has no right to whisper into our minds to challenge our identity in Jesus and bring condemnation and accusation. We have a right to stand against these negative beliefs and take authority over them in Jesus name. Speaking in our prayer language can be important in this context.

Jesus asked the man at the pool of Bethesda, *"Do you want to be made whole?"* (John 5:6-9) The man asked Jesus to help him. As we ask for help, He will be there with us through the power of the Holy Spirit because the weapons we have are mighty through God and we can overcome.

This is not the time to back away and rebuild walls. It is a time to press through, dealing with the fears, the pride and self-preservation, and coming into and staying in a place of freedom in our minds.

We have looked before at how our beliefs are established very early in life and how out of those beliefs, habits and patterns are formed.

Having looked at negative behaviour cycles, we will now look at positive ones.

POSITIVE BEHAVIOUR CYCLES OR PATTERNS

The challenge is to live in a Godly cycle where acceptance releases a security that through the Holy Spirit gives a sense of daily achievement. This cycle is the essence of that.

THE FATHER HEART OF GOD

This is where we start. We do need a revelation of this truth and Jesus was so clear in his response to the Father and this gives us great impetus and hope. We know acceptance starts here.

Acceptance - This is offered out of the revelation of the Father's heart. We are *'accepted in the beloved'* (Ephesians 1:6). In Christ, adopted *'into the family of God'* (Romans 8:15). Justified through grace by faith. We know and feel it and live it! We can declare, "I am accepted, and I am acceptable."

Satisfaction - Here is the sense of the fullness of the Spirit, the God of hope filling us with all joy and peace, knowing the power of the Spirit to live daily, abiding in the vine and entering into spiritual disciplines.

Status - I am a son, by birth, by blood.

'When all the people were baptized, it came to pass that Jesus also was baptized; and while He prayed, the heaven was opened. And the Holy Spirit

descended in bodily form like a dove upon Him, and a voice came from heaven which said, "You are My beloved Son; in You I am well pleased" (Luke 3:21-22). Jesus knew who he was and so can we.

Achievement - We can discover a sense of achievement in fulfilling God's purpose in our lives. We are His workmanship, His work of art (Ephesians 2:10).

A Cycle of Acceptance:

Security in who I am in God

Humility

Fulfilment

Enjoyment / Pleasure

Relationship / Acceptance

A Pattern of Behaviour To Aim For:

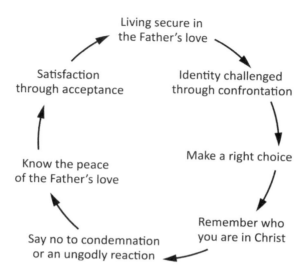

MEMORY POINTS

- Learn to control your mind and not allow your mind to control you.
- Refuse to let your past shape your future.
- Rejection will always affect us but it is how we handle it that is important.
- We can change the way we look at things.
- Beliefs become habits and habits can be broken.
- Belief systems dictate how we perceive ourselves.
- Patterns of behaviour develop from belief systems.
- We can change our beliefs by challenging them.
- Do not cherish negative thoughts.
- Keynote scripture 2 Corinthians 10:4-5.
- As we change we can live in a Godly pattern of behaviour.
- Do not think you are; know you are.

TOWARDS RECOVERY

Recovery is a process for anyone working towards freedom from rejection. It is being able to know, and continue to know, the sense of belonging that motivates a person day by day, giving identity and destiny.

JOSEPH

Although Joseph went through tremendous rejection and brought some of it upon himself, God was faithful to him and he came through into a place that was crucial for the destiny of his people (Genesis 37-46).

Being a favourite is one thing, but having the best coat and acting in a superior way, despite the fact that you are almost the youngest in the family is another. *'Now Israel loved Joseph more than all his children, because he was the son of his old age. Also he made him a tunic of many colours. But when his brothers saw that their father loved him more than all his brothers, they hated him and could not speak peaceably to him'* (Genesis 37:3-4).

Joseph also had two prophetic dreams, that made his brothers even more angry and even his father rebuked him. The message in the dream was that the whole family were to bow down to him in an attitude of subservience

(Genesis 37:5-11). The untimely interpretation of the dreams, together with Joseph's arrogance, made the brothers jealous and ultimately they decided to get rid of him. They put Joseph in a pit then sold him as a slave and he eventually found himself working in an Egyptian home. He was falsely accused of sexual immorality and put in prison. Although God was with him his family and friends forgot him.

Rejection from your family is devastating and destructive, and so many feel they can identify with Joseph in his betrayal, abandonment and isolation. Rejected people can identify with the pit, slavery, false accusation, prison and feeling forgotten. We need to be aware, though of the reality of our own personal situations, and be careful and discerning in the way we apply these issues.

Eventually Joseph was remembered and this now mature and secure man was taken into the royal court to interpret Pharaoh's dream. The interpretation pleased Pharaoh and he asked Joseph to prepare a plan that would save the Egyptian people. Pharaoh put Joseph in charge of the whole of Egypt. As the famine hit the rest of the world, Joseph's family became hungry and finally made the journey to Egypt for food. The dreams of many years ago were beginning to come to pass.

When Joseph saw his brothers the memories returned and even though twenty years had passed the pain was still very strong. The brothers did not recognise Joseph until he revealed to them who he was. Reconciliation came with many tears and when, at last, Jacob came to Egypt, restoration of the whole family took place. An amazing miracle happened after many years of rejection and separation. The purpose of God not only brought the family together but also saved many Nations because the famine was worldwide. (Genesis 41:56-57).

There is a scripture that shows how God brought good out of such a bad situation. Joseph said to his brothers, *"You intended to harm me, but God intended it for good to accomplish what is now being done, the saving of many lives"* (Genesis 50:20).

God intervened with a plan, which was the bigger picture and for the greater good. He wanted to save as many lives as possible, so He took the good out of a desperate situation. Joseph was thrust into Pharaoh's court with revelation and a word of wisdom, to bring an answer to the famine that was coming. Joseph seemed to have lost everything, yet God led him into his destiny and the fulfilment of his earlier dreams. In the midst of the pain and rejection God took the good out of each experience and used it to fulfil His purposes.

Joseph's recovery was such that he responded in love to his brothers, *"No, do not be afraid. I will continue to take care of you and your children. So he reassured them by speaking kindly to them"* (Genesis 50:21).

SUMMARY

There is a much bigger question that needs to be considered: was the strategy of God to plan the demise of Joseph and then receive the glory for rescuing him or did He allow it? Were God's hands tied because of the freewill response of man? Was the enemy behind this? Did Satan manipulate things to bring destruction in order to undermine and bring down the purposes of God?

How does this affect us in our rejection? Did God plan for us to go through rejection, in order to bring us out of it for His glory?

The answer is no to all of these questions because our God is not that kind of God. He loves us and accepts us and would not deliberately put us through such difficult circumstances, so that we would be manipulated to love Him more. We love Him because we choose to. We need to be aware of the irresponsibility of humanity and the fact that we have an enemy, who will work in any way he can to bring destruction into our lives. Our loving Heavenly Father's purpose is for everything including our pain and rejection, to ultimately work for our good and not for evil.

Jesus told a parable about weeds where good seed was sown, but an enemy of the man who had sown the seed came and sowed tares. He said, *"an enemy has done this"* (Matthew 13:24-30). We have an enemy too.

Joseph finally saw the hand of God clearly in his life and circumstances and so can we.

This is summed up in the New Testament, *'and we know that God causes everything to work together for the good of those who love God and are called according to His purpose for them'* (Romans 8:28).

'Do you think anyone is going to be able to drive a wedge between us and Christ's love for us? There is no way! Not trouble, not hard times, not hatred, not hunger, not homelessness, not bullying threats, not backstabbing, not even the worst sins listed in Scripture. None of this fazes us because Jesus loves us. I'm absolutely convinced that nothing - nothing living or dead, angelic or demonic, today or tomorrow, high or low, thinkable or unthinkable - absolutely nothing can get between us and God's love because of the way that Jesus our Master has embraced us' (Romans 8:35, 37-39 MESSAGE).

God is good; God is safe and God is certainly reliable!

RISKY LIVING

It is vital that we see there is a way forward beyond rejection. This does not mean there will never be any more rejection, but the challenge is how we handle what comes to us or is imposed on us.

It is also important to understand that we have a major part to play in the ongoing circumstances of life. We have everything to do with what is going on in our lives and we have an ability to exercise right and Godly control over the issues we face.

With this in mind, we need to consider the perspective of our God given right to make choices and how we should exercise our will in the power of the Holy Spirit. Our goal is to develop and grow into a stronger relationship with our Father God.

The area of making good and right choices is often neglected in Christian circles, with many of us wanting a quick healing and/or deliverance. This often speaks of irresponsibility and denial.

It is important to make sure that pastoral care follows on from prayer ministry. After ministry, people need support to understand and adjust to change. Some however want the prayer but not the discipleship. Maybe we think the enemy will not bother us again so we neglect the basic disciplines we need to move away from rejection and into maturity in our walk with Jesus. Part of the role of the church is to disciple, and in this context the church needs to own its responsibility.

Planning ahead is crucial after a time of prayer. Moving on will need wise management and this means good and honest relationships and a willingness to talk and pray things through. Being alone is not the answer, but planning together is the way forward. Consider what is necessary in your own life to maintain the counsel, healing and deliverance received. It is sensible that you plan certain times when you can report on how you are feeling, assess strengths and weaknesses and pray together. If you know the care is continuing and that you have good access to it, you will be secure enough to press forward. If the person who originally prayed with you is not able to continue with you in care, make sure that there is someone in your local church who is available. Check this out with your leaders or others you trust. Do not remain alone hoping things might turn out to be better.

Once you have had a pastoral assessment get down to the specifics. There will be disciplines and you need to understand your responsibility in carrying them out. It is important to have something to aim for because discipleship and growth does not just happen.

Restoration and recovery are important in the process of living in freedom from rejection.

RESTORATION

Restoration or rehabilitation is a process of helping an individual achieve the best quality of life possible. Basically, it is to make fit again or to restore to good condition. In the context of rejection it means to re-establish esteem or to give back what was lost or taken, or to restore to a rightful place.

A prime example of someone working towards recovery is Mephibosheth (2 Samuel 9:1-13). We saw in previous chapters that he finally came to a place where he had to make a right choice. King David had made a life-changing offer to him and in order to begin to get on the road to recovery, Mephibosheth needed to choose to accept the offer. He sat at the King's table, which meant he was with the family on a regular and consistent basis. Rehabilitation meant being accepted and restoration was giving Mephibosheth the right place, which ultimately led to recovery.

RECOVERY

Alcoholics who have stopped drinking alcohol are known as recovering alcoholics however long it was since the last time they drank alcohol because they are in a continual recovery.

The power of rejection is mostly outside of the control of the rejected person. The premise is that a person will never stop being rejected because the rejection usually comes from others. You cannot say you have been set free from rejection or you have been healed from rejection and will never be rejected again: it does not work like that. The issue is being so healed on the inside, that when rejection comes in its various forms, we actually see it coming. We will be able to perceive and understand what is going on before it affects us or if it does we will handle it in a different way than before and hence protect ourselves and overcome.

Recovery is the consistent and continual process of restoration whereby we regain possession and Godly control of the way we are, the way we think and the way we behave as secure people in daily life. We need to learn how to live with rejection around us without letting it affect us.

We have seen that the power of the mind and our belief and behaviour patterns are crucial in all of this. We can know deliverance from the demonic related to rejection. We can then learn how to live without the demonic power affecting or oppressing us, and live in the power of the Holy Spirit who gives us ability to think in a right and Godly way.

HOW JESUS HANDLED REJECTION

Throughout His life Jesus experienced the personal pain of rejection even in His home town but:

- He continued to reach out to the people with His Father's love and if necessary heal them.
- He carried on with His ministry in towns and villages proclaiming the Kingdom of God.
- He knew who He was and what His purpose in life was.
- He was secure in His Fathers love.
- His self-worth, value and self-esteem were strong.

It is worth considering:

- He did not question who He was.
- He did not defend Himself.
- He did not react in anger.
- He did not let rejection affect Him.

We can follow Jesus in these ways.

- We can let God not other people determine our worth.
- We can admit when rejection hurts without having a pity party. It is a challenge to admit you are hurt and then get on with living purposefully.
- We can reach out to those in need and touch them with God's love.
- We can move into our destiny in Him and keep on serving Him and others. No matter who we are we have a scriptural mandate, *"for I can do everything through Christ, who gives me strength"* (Philippians 4:13).

Jesus had a great ability to embrace rejection and not allow it to affect him. When He was at His hometown, Nazareth, Jesus was amazed at the unbelief of the people. *'And because of their unbelief, He could not do any mighty miracles among them except to place His hands on a few sick people and heal them. And He was amazed at their unbelief'* (Mark 6:5-6). Their deep-seated unbelief, contempt and scoffing was a strong rejection, which restricted Jesus in what He could do there. The way He responded was to face the rejection and embrace it. There is healing in facing up to rejection. Choosing to embrace it sets you free.

The only other time the word amazed is used in the Gospels was where Jesus was amazed at someone's faith and this was a Gentile, a Roman Centurion (Luke 7:9). In the first narrative the people in Nazareth showed a dramatic lack of faith, when Jesus probably would have expected to see it.

In this context, He would not have expected a Gentile to have faith, so when He saw it, He was amazed. This was an expression of acceptance and Jesus embraced it. He said He had not found such great faith even in Israel. The result was that a miracle came out of the humility and faith of someone the Jews rejected. The Centurion's servant was healed.

Do we believe our doubts and doubt our beliefs or do we believe our beliefs and doubt our doubts? There is power in unbelief.

RECOGNISABLE PATTERNS OF ACCEPTANCE AND REJECTION

Our perceptions affect the way we live and it is crucial we are consistently aware of them. The only way to recognise those patterns of behaviour is to be vulnerable and honest. When the enemy tries to damage and suffocate us with his lies, how we see and understand God's truth will counteract it.

By responding to Satan's manipulative words, we believe a lie just as Adam and Eve did in the garden. We begin to think that God does not have our best interest at heart and that He has withdrawn from us, because we do not reach His standards. It is as though God has withheld good things from us until we do something to gain acceptance.

Satan will attempt to control rejected people by getting them to develop all sorts of defence systems and attack strategies to block pain and to gain significance. They suppress emotions, are compulsive perfectionists, drive themselves to succeed, withdraw and be passive, attack those who hurt, punish themselves when there is failure, say clever or funny things to be accepted or help others so that they themselves will be appreciated. The truth is that life is lived in a world filled with pain, hurts and rejection. Yet since the fall, man has looked to others rather than God for his pressing need of self-worth. "I am who others say I am," "my value is in their opinion of me." So, we become dominated by our performance and ability to please others and, consequently, have difficulty in recognising our true identity in

Christ. Often we have developed what is known as a 'have to' mentality: "I have to do well, I have to look good, I have to be liked." Jesus did not have to be successful or have to please anyone to have a healthy sense of worth, value and esteem. So where is our true value based? Is it on our behaviour, on the approval of others or on what God's word says? The deceptive lies of Satan are designed to ensure that we are worn down until we feel far away from God's unfailing love and become 'restless wanderers' (Genesis 4:12).

We can identify Satan's lies because we know God's truth. God accepts me because He loves me unconditionally.

SATAN'S LIE

As we move into restoration and recovery from rejection it is crucial we continue to be aware of the ploy of the enemy. Do we really think Satan will give up on us? We will have times of blessing but remember we still can be trapped by the enemy's lies. We need to consistently discern and understand that Satan, even though he has no right, will try to control us with his lies. Let us declare that we will not let him do that.

It is necessary to consider the following:

Hopelessness:
"I am what I am."
"I am made this way."
"I cannot change."
"Everything is hopeless."

Too often our sense of self-image rests on our perception of our past. However by the grace of God and the power of the Spirit working in our lives we can change.

The challenge we face is to let go of the past. We must release the old to fully come into the new so that we will not be controlled by yesterday's memories. It is like hanging on to a trapeze, which is our security until another trapeze appears. This trapeze is the way forward and we have a choice to make. To hold the new trapeze we must release the old. Will we let go of the past in order to enter into our destiny?

APPROVAL

"I must be accepted by others to feel good about myself."

How do we think others see or perceive us? Most of us would be wrong in our assessment.

It has been said that rejection is the type of communication that says someone is unsatisfactory; they do not measure up to our standard. It speaks of low value, disrespect, and a lack of appreciation. The fear of rejection can therefore dominate our lives because no one wants to be rejected, and once you have been or felt rejected, fear of the next time may haunt you. We know that rejection is a very effective and destructive tool. People may even have used rejection to try to motivate. The love of Jesus never uses condemnation or guilt to bring us to a place of response.

Fear of rejection will control us to the extent that we base our self-worth on the opinions of others, rather than on our relationship with God. Depending on others for our worth and value will enslave us, and we will lose something of our right to Sonship. The approval of others will never bring complete satisfaction.

Punishment:
"I do not deserve to be loved because I am a failure."
"I messed up. I will be blamed and I deserve it!"

From a rejection mind-set it is easy to condemn failure, especially your own.

The perception is that anyone who fails is unworthy of love and deserves to be punished. In response to failure a person may retreat into isolation and depression or blame shift. Blaming someone else does not help; it just increases the guilt and fear of rejection.

Remember one of the roots of rejection is self-rejection and the taunts of condemnation from the enemy reinforce it. We will begin to close down, lose touch with Father God and build up our own protection.

In situations like this frustration with ourselves turns to anger, which will either make us want to hurt ourselves or hurt other people.

Performance:
"I have to meet certain standards and perform well to feel good."

Deception will make me think that if I do well, if I succeed, I will be happy. If I think that I can measure up to the right standard, I will feel good about myself.

Despite a measure of competence in certain areas, perfectionism will ensure that I still fear rejection, despair, failure, react defensively to criticism, and want to control most, if not all situations. If I have to meet certain standards, I will tend to live by rules. This will become a trap. My past failures will torment me. I will try harder and the pressure will get greater, as I become even more controlled by my rules.

GOD'S TRUTH

Moving forward towards recovery and wholeness involves accepting God's truth in place of Satan's lies.

The following four areas are essential to consider. Begin to absorb them, because even though you may be aware of them, do you really know them and live as though they are part of you? Remember Jesus said to Satan, 'Man does not live by bread alone but by every word that comes from the mouth of God' (Luke 4:4, Deuteronomy 8:3).

- "I am complete in Christ."
- "I am accepted by God."
- "I am loved by God."
- "I am forgiven and God is pleased with me."

Can you identify Satan's lies, which become false beliefs and recognise and begin to believe what God says?

The Apostle Paul declares not a truth but the truth, which is our starting point. *'Not that I already obtained this or have already reached the goal; but I press on to make it my own, because Christ Jesus has made me his own'* (Philippians 3:12).

Do Not Let Rejection Define You

Living a lifestyle sourced in rejection, means you may believe that the rejection reflects the sum total of your worth as a person and you decide that it hurts so much you will never take a risk again. Playing the rejection over and over again in your mind keeps it alive and that may lead to you to have a large and ongoing pity party, even though you are the only guest. You will probably believe that everyone knows about you, are looking at you and are talking about you. It is easy to get stuck, stay focused on the rejection and never even consider moving forward.

Memory Points

- We may be healed but we are never perfect.
- God meant it for good.
- Risk is a walk of faith as we live in God.

- Finally Mephibosheth was restored.
- Restoration is the beginning of a process for us to live in recovery.
- Jesus experienced rejection, understood rejection and handled rejection; so can we.
- The patterns of rejection are a lie of Satan.
- The patterns of acceptance are God's truth. Choose well.
- Once we allowed rejection to define us: Now we can say 'No.'

LIVING IN RECOVERY

There will always be problems, difficulties and challenges in life and how we respond to what happens, the way we see the situation and the way we see ourselves in it is obviously important.

The almost total disaster David and his army walked into was at the top of the scale. It was horrendous yet in the midst of such desperation, the way he responded gives us hope. We may think our situation is not as bad as this but, the point is, we can see how David took action in the face of such difficulty and we can learn from it.

ZIGLAG

Ziglag was a town in the south of Judah where David and his army lived. David and his men had returned to Ziglag on the third day and found the Amalekites had attacked it, burned it and had taken captive all of the families that were there (1 Samuel 30:1-2). This brought David and his men into a terrible crisis. After weeping deeply some of the men turned on David and talked about stoning him. They were so bitter and full of pain.

How did David handle the conflict and rejection, which could have easily led to him being killed by his own men? This was not opposition from his enemies; it was from his loyal men who were his friends! It seemed there was no hope.

David did something that was simply amazing because in this desperate situation it would have been easy to run, blame others or turn his back on God but he stood his ground and *'encouraged and strengthened himself in the Lord his God'* (1 Samuel 30:6).

Discouragement can be defined as 'anything that makes us less confident and hopeful.' Another way to look at it, is to say that encouragement is the act of putting courage into someone. Therefore, discouragement is anything that undermines courage.

This is something we need to look at in our process of recovery, because conflict will happen, and there is a better way than to fall back into rejection. The fact that David in his isolation, loneliness and discouragement was able to find God and be strengthened as he responded to Him is quite astonishing. We can do the same.

David had a good relationship with God and was able to trust Him. Throughout the Psalms David declares the Lord to be his strength and shield, his rock in whom he takes refuge, his fortress and his deliverer (Psalm 18:1-3, Psalm 28:7). The Lord became his hiding place (Psalm 32:7). David was able to lift up his eyes to the hills and ask where his help came from, and immediately he knew it came from the Lord (Psalm 121:1-2).

David made a right choice regarding despair, guilt and regret; there was no transfer of blame, feelings rejection or self-rejection. We see great resilience and courage as he trusted in his God. There was something almost automatic that happened when David faced trouble, which came out of his consistent relationship with God.

David strengthened himself in God. In fact, David had a word with himself! *"Why am I so discouraged? Why is my heart sad? I will put my hope in God. I will praise Him again my Saviour and my God. Now I am deeply discouraged but I will remember you"* (Psalm 42:5). He actually repeated this (Psalm 43:5), which underlines the importance of the issue.

Do we passively wait for God or do we by faith make a choice to receive His strength? I think we know what to do.

As David turned to God and found His strength, a confidence came in the midst of the pain and he was able to ask God for help and direction. Everything was restored, all the people abducted were brought home and nothing was lost (1 Samuel 30:18-19).

It is significant that David and his men returned to Ziglag on the third day. The third day is mentioned many times throughout scripture and it symbolises divine intervention and resurrection. To have that phrase inserted in the text is so meaningful as it signifies hope even in the most desperate of times. As David strengthened himself in God, so can we. Knowing that Jesus has overcome death and the enemy makes us *'more than conquerors'* and that *'nothing will separate us from the love of God'* (Romans 8:37-39).

The crisis at Ziglag was turned into an opportunity and because of David's response to God there was restoration of all that was lost. 'We know that in all things God works for the good of those who love Him' (Romans 8:28). Our wonderful God has this amazing ability to take the good out of the bad and the positive out of the negative. His purpose is to not only be with us when times are difficult, but also take the best out of those situations so that we can trust Him and look at the bigger picture.

In the conflicts we face, as we go through the process of recovery, we have choices to make. Are we going to let rejection control us as it did in the past or are we going to strengthen ourselves in God and receive a new confidence to move ahead?

Remember we are always acceptable to God and we always have access to Him. His acceptance of us is unconditional because it is impossible for us to earn it, deserve it or be entitled to it. God is good; He will not fail us. Amidst the desperate situation that David was in, he knew that God was with him to sustain him, strengthen him and give him a way out. God has not changed.

HANDLING CONFLICT

Understanding how to handle conflict is important in building relationships. Conflict usually happens through a difference of opinion, which may lead to a dispute and ultimately a collision of personalities. We are not immune from conflict; it happens. How rejected people in recovery handle this is important. How we communicate with each other determines what kind of relationships we build. Wrong reactions may cause loss of trust. The way we communicate is important and understanding what confrontation really means is priority. We need to be aware of the way we understand each other and what we say and how we say it. Be aware too of any preconceptions we may have, as it is important to be prepared to be flexible. Disagreement is not wrong; attitude and wrong use of emotions could be. Having a lack of understanding of a situation or person will affect the relationship. Therefore it is important to be aware of the full facts in any situation so that the problem is confronted fairly and resolved in a Godly way.

There are many different personality types and it is important to be aware of how we handle communication appropriately. If we make the wrong assumptions about people before we know them we will soon have conflict. We need to be discerning and careful avoiding presuppositions and preconceptions.

A long time ago we had some very good teaching on understanding and building relationships. I have used some of this and adapted it to focus on rejection.

In principle, relationship tends to be built in three stages:

Veneer - Rejected people tend to be surface people. They give a distorted picture of who they are, covering up the real person. They relate out of self-protection not allowing themselves close friendships in case they are rejected. They live with fear of rejection.

Disillusionment - When we see that our friendships are going wrong, disenchantment sets in. We feel disheartened and disappointed and revert to veneer to hide and self-protect.

Reality - It is possible to reach a point where we break through disillusionment into reality. Self-confidence, value and worth are strong and even though we are seen as we really are, it does not matter. We make right choices not to fall back into the rejection cycle, because we are living in our healing and therefore relationships become real and authentic.

Rejected people tend to stay in a cycle of veneer and disillusionment and never break through into reality.

Rather than reacting in a challenging situation where all the rejection buttons are pressed it is important to learn to take a step back and find a healthy and Godly response. This will not be easy at first but, with practice and perseverance, things will change.

We have options as conflict faces us, and it is up to us to make the right choices. To self-protect, a rejected person would probably respond in this way:

> I will get him/her - A need for revenge.
> I will get out - I am afraid so I will escape.
> I will give in - It is better to comply because I need your friendship.
> I will meet halfway - Compromise is the easiest way out.

Behaving in this way will never resolve conflict.

However there is another way:

Care enough to confront - I want a relationship but I also want integrity and honesty. I care enough to be honest and to give respect. To care is a concern about another's wellbeing and a desire to put things right. To confront is to talk face to face without avoiding the issue or showing hostility: to communicate in love with minimum threat and stress.

In our communications with one another, we need to continually be caring enough to face up to things. Conflict should be seen as a means to an end - peace. We need to learn not to avoid conflict because we are afraid! We do know that 'perfect love casts out fear' (1John 4:18).

We need to confront with truth and affirm with love. The two ingredients to cultivate any relationship with integrity are truth and love.

> Truth with love brings healing.
> Truth told in love enables us to grow.
> Truth expressed in love produces change.

All positive relationships begin with friendship, appreciation and respect. What can we build that we know will last if there is no trust wrapped in love and truth? *'Care as much about each other as yourselves'* (Romans 12:16).

Being Vulnerable - Vulnerability is an enemy of rejection. Being vulnerable is the last thing a rejected person would allow him or herself to be.

The root of the word is to wound. To be vulnerable is to be exposed to the possibility of being wounded, attacked or harmed, physically, emotionally and spiritually. Would a person affected by rejection allow himself or herself to be exposed like that? In our relationships, we need to be vulnerable as an equal amongst equals, which means no self-protection, no hiding or putting up walls to feel secure.

Being vulnerable is not being:

Angry - Anger is used intentionally or unintentionally to control a person or situation and can therefore make people fearful. Angry people react against any threat to their own preservation because, actually, what they want is recognition and acceptance of who they are. In their insecurity they chose to become angry as a defence to the perceived threat. It is easy to get angry, lash back, feel very hurt and withdraw. They need a recognition of their worth, but in this state, they actually reject and ignore the very person they want to be loved by.

Who makes you angry? The first reaction is to blame someone else, but the truth is that you make yourself angry. Perhaps it is easier to blame someone else, but we are responsible for how we react.

Jesus was very clear about the two great commandments. The second one is, *"love your neighbour as yourself"* (Matthew 22:39). As much as you love yourself you love your neighbour. Surely the same principle applies to anger. If you are angry with your neighbour this means you are angry with yourself.

Anxious - This has been described as an extreme uneasiness of the mind or a great sense of uncertainty, agitation, or even a dread, or brooding fear, about some situation. Severe anxiety is definitely not good news, and will afflict rather than affect a person vulnerable to rejection. It is easy to let your thoughts of how you think others perceive you get out of hand. Often the issue is never the issue and we need to learn to discern and symptom watch. Vulnerability means resting in the peace of God instead of letting rejection control the situation.

Being vulnerable is being able to:

Listen - Listening is such a key component in building relationships. How do we listen? We need to learn to focus on the person who is speaking without getting distracted and certainly without interrupting. We have all opened our hearts to others and before we finish they interrupt, highjack the conversation and start talking about their problems. *"Answering before listening is both stupid and rude"* (Proverbs 18:13 MESSAGE). The person we are in conversation with needs to know that we are giving them our full attention. How much do we really hear? When we move on to something else it is easy, to forget what we have heard. We need to be able to understand the feelings and hurts of others. I want to learn to hear what the person wants to tell me as I listen. I want to learn to go beyond anything that may hurt, reject, or threaten me but I also want to trust others to hear my feelings and viewpoint. The way we listen to God will help us to listen to each other. *"Understand this, my dear brothers and sisters: You must all be quick to listen, slow to speak, and slow to get angry"* (James 1:19).

Trust - Rejected people do not fully understand trust as they have rarely experienced it because of past hurts. Trust is basically having confidence in a person. When you trust people you have confidence in them, in their integrity, their reliability and their honesty. There will be no suspicion of any personal agenda or motive.

When people say, "I cannot trust" are they really saying they will not trust? We have to be open and honest and be prepared to take risks because we are basically letting a part of our lives go out of control and into the hands of someone else and the outcome depends on that person and not us.

We all know that trust is fragile. It is possible for forgiveness to happen in a moment but trust has to grow. We can get to the place where we trust again because of our relationship with our loving Heavenly Father and we trust Him.

Make Peace - There is a difference between making the peace and keeping the peace. Are we peacekeepers or peacemakers? Surely our goal is to move from keeping the peace, which is keeping silent and keeping out of the way, and move towards making peace, which is being reconciled with someone. Some of us have put so much under the carpet we, keep falling over the mountain we have created. Those that have experienced rejection know how to run away, but the challenge to us is to face up to things and people. This means to care for, confront and value people with humility so that the past is faced properly and the future is secured. Peacemakers take responsibility for making decisions according to their own conscience, in the peace of God. *"You are blessed when you can show people how to cooperate instead of compete or fight. That's when you discover who you really are and your place in God's family"* (Matthew 5:9 MESSAGE). Peacemakers are risk takers; they look at other people and not themselves.

Be Assertive - This means neither being passive or aggressive. In family fun and banter, my daughters will tell us if we are being PA (passive aggressive). This is verbal or non-verbal communication, intentionally masking true feelings.

Passivity is not having the confidence in a relationship to express your honest feelings, thoughts or beliefs. Being passive means you do not take responsibility for your feelings, but you allow them to fester and you build walls of self-protection and hide.

Aggression is when we stand up for our rights in a way that will override others. You say what you want, think and feel at the expense of others. There are hidden agendas, loaded words, statements that label and blame with threats and accusations. You act in a superior way with a loud and demanding voice, which dominates and even humiliates. Later you may feel embarrassed or selfish. People will feel degraded, depreciated, rejected and hurt by you and may become defensive, angry or both and will resent, distrust and fear you.

Being assertive is expressing how you feel, but not violating others. You respect others as you communicate. You communicate honestly, and confidently and you listen closely in a relaxed manner. The goal is to give and receive respect. As you grow in this, self confidence improves, physical distress dissolves, and people feel respected and valued. In the kingdom of God being direct and honest is vital as long as it is undergirded by mercy and grace.

FIGHT, FLIGHT OR FREEZE - IS THERE ANOTHER WAY

Conflict will trigger a reaction of fight or flight, which usually begins with a stress reaction, either mentally or physically. This internal reaction prepares the body to either stay and deal with the threatening circumstance or run away to safety. The body activates automatically, becoming tense as the heart rate begins to increase, blood pressure rises and breathing becomes appreciably faster.

A way of looking at this is the example of a caveman confronted by a ferocious animal. Automatically the whole body is mobilised for action; energy is concentrated. The bodily functions change to confront the situation, with the adrenalin flowing so that maximum energy is ready to be used. The caveman will either fight the animal, turn and run to the nearest tree, or freeze with fear and be killed. The bodily system works well in the face of real danger.

However today there are not usually any wild animals to chase or be chased by, but it is clear that the same bodily functions happen. Often it is in very difficult situations of conflict that you may want to fight, run away or freeze. However you cannot kill the animal or run up a tree, so it is inside yourself that something happens. You may try to take control of the problem by reacting in either a passive or aggressive manner.

The anger or fears connected may not necessarily be conscious, but at times they are triggered and overflow, or leak out of the emotions. You may be physically affected, but what happens inside is equally important as defence mechanisms automatically gather up the pain, the hurts and wounds and they become hidden in the unconscious.

Both fight and flight are aggressive weapons. Fight is often motivated by anger, which can be expressed by criticism, sarcasm or pride. Flight can be motivated by fear leading to depression, inner vows, denial, self-pity or self-centredness.

With regard to freezing, we considered earlier in the book 'Frozen Memories' (Page 195) and 'Mind Games' (Page 215). If necessary go back and remind yourself of the importance of understanding these vital issues because they lead to the ultimate place of freedom.

Freedom is what we are aiming for. This is the place where we can live in peace with God, with ourselves, because of who we are in Christ and with others. *"You will know the truth and the truth will set you free"* (John 8:32). The amazing fact is that we can know Jesus and be accepted for He is truth, and for that reason we live in a freedom that will continually be with us as we move on in recovery.

GOD IS ENOUGH

There is an excellent scripture underlining the fact that God is enough and it is the sort of encouraging word that can sustain us when we are in difficult circumstances.

"Now to Him who is able to do exceedingly abundantly above all that we ask or think, according to the power that works in us, to Him be glory in the church by Christ Jesus to all generations, forever and ever. Amen" (Ephesians 3:20-21).

What God is saying is that He can do anything and far more than we can ever imagine, even in our wildest dreams, and He does it by the power of His Spirit who works in us. God is able, for His power has no limit; it is infinite. This means it is vastly more than more. He is able to go beyond the beyond and continue far beyond anything that we can conceive. In fact in our measured thinking, it becomes more than we could ever measure. God cannot only do more than we ask, more than we think and more than we can ever dream, even in the wildest sense, but He is exceedingly abundantly more.

However there is a condition that involves us. God invites us to join with Him in the release of this promise but, in joining with Him, we have to recognise that we have some responsibility in this too because it is according to the power that works in us.

God in His wisdom is committed to use frail, flawed and broken people like us to release His power. This is the amazing love that the Father has for us. He is not afraid to come down to where we are and to elevate us to where He is. Through His unconditional love to us He has given His Spirit to empower us. This is God wanting to work His works through us. It is limitless, boundless, broad enough to encompass everything and deep enough to reach us.

What can there be higher than the fullness of God? It is logical to ask how this can be true. How can something so far above us ever become reality in our lives? It can only happen through Him who is able to do exceeding abundantly above all that we ask or think. I call it amazing grace.

The mother of one of the greatest film stars ever, Audrey Hepburn, said to her, "You've done quite well seeing you've got no talent." It is words like this that can destroy not just a career, but also a life. Whatever has been spoken into us, we can still live in the reality that God is enough.

Hope In The Valley Of Achor

For so many rejected people hope is as an oasis in the wilderness of indecision and insecurity. Biblical hope is defined as eager expectation or anticipation, and is certainly not the doubt and uncertainty of a world-view that is prevalent. God gives us great comfort through His word.

"Therefore, behold, I will allure her, I will bring her into the wilderness, and speak comfort to her. I will give her back her vineyards from there, and the Valley of Achor as a door of hope; she shall sing there, as in the days of her youth, as in the day when she came up from the land of Egypt" (Hosea 2:14-15).

What God is saying is that He will attract and captivate His people with His love and words of comfort. He wants to reassure us, to put us at ease as He speaks tenderly and affectionately to us. His promise is for peace and fruitfulness in our lives, with healing taking place in our mind, emotions and spirit. He will return what has been taken from us, but most of all He will transform the Valley of Achor into a gateway of hope. When we realise that Achor means trouble, the whole things makes sense.

It does not take much to talk about the trouble that rejection has caused in our lives but God is providing a way out. This is a promise of restoration through the tender heart of the Father's love. Interestingly Achor was known as a fruitful valley and, once again, the door will be open to better days where we can sing as maybe we once did. Rejection and singing are not really compatible but our God is a God of the impossible. You can sing about coming out of your Egypt, which is your point of deliverance and healing.

'Who is this coming out of the wilderness leaning on her beloved?' (Song of Songs 8:5) It is you and I leaning on Him and walking together. We are not alone. As Moses spoke to Joshua about going into the land of promise,

God would say to you, *"so be strong and courageous! Do not be afraid and do not panic before them. For the Lord your God will personally go ahead of you. He will neither fail you nor abandon you"* (Deuteronomy 31:6 NLT).

FINALLY

There can be a restoration of first love.

"God showed how much he loved us by sending his one and only Son into the world so that we might have eternal life through him. This is real love— not that we loved God, but that he loved us and sent his Son as a sacrifice to take away our sins" (1 John 4:9-10 NLT).

"Let us therefore love Him, because He first loved us" (1 John 4:19 NLT).

God's first love means He loves us above and before anything. The essence of the gospel is God so loved all mankind that He was willing to sacrifice His own son. *"See how very much our Father loves us, for He calls us His children, and that is what we are"* (1 John 3:1).

God has not left us in any doubt regarding His love to us. He loves us with perfect love.

For various reasons some people have lost their first love and rejected people desperately long to receive and to give away unfailing love.
Jesus had an accusation against that magnificent and gifted church Ephesus, *"I hold this against you: You have lost or forsaken your first love"* (Revelation 2:4).

There was little ardour or passion; enthusiasm and fervour had gone into decline. Remember the two disciples when they realised Jesus had been with them? 'They said to each other, *"didn't our hearts burn within us as he talked with us on the road and explained the Scriptures to us?"'* (Luke 24:32)

Their hearts began to glow again with that intense love because they had been with Jesus. They were fired up!

Are we losing Him as First Love or are we losing our love for Him. First love could be another name for Him. He is my first love but maybe you have never met Him. Maybe rejection has been a barrier for you finding Him, even from the beginning of your life. A key to being released from the pain of rejection is to grasp hold of God's grace and open yourself to His love, so that the Holy Spirit can pour that love into your heart and out of that abounding love, a relationship with Him will begin, and you will have a new sense of confidence, value and esteem.

Memory Points

Mother Teresa said, 'the biggest disease today isn't leprosy or cancer. It's the feeling of being uncared for, unwanted, loneliness or being abandoned.' This is the impetus for us to move on into full recovery from rejection.

- 'There is no pain worse than rejection and no delight greater than acceptance.'
- Was Ziglag a crisis or did it become an opportunity?
- We can learn how to strengthen ourselves in God.
- Even in the difficult times, the joy of the Lord is our strength (Nehemiah 8:10).
- Getting to reality in our relationships with each other is vital.
- We can get to the place where we confront with truth and affirm with love.
- Being vulnerable will challenge rejection.
- Concentrate on listening, trusting, making peace and being assertive.
- We can express how we feel in a way that does not violate others.
- Instead of fight, flight or freeze there is another way.
- God is enough and God is reliable and He is able to do far more

than we can ever think of.

- There is always hope in the Valley of Achor.
- Remember our foundation of life in God is first love. Everything grows out of that.
- Have we lost our first love for Him?
- He is our first love.

APPENDIX 1

THE FRUIT OF REJECTION

I want to introduce you to the three lists of words, which I consider to be fruit and describe the three roots of rejection. The more you are able to relate these words to your own character and personality, the more a picture emerges, which gives an indication of the root of rejection. For example look at the word insecurity, which means a lacking in confidence in situations, unsure or unstable. If that is a weakness in character, it may alongside other key words highlight the possibility of a root of self-rejection. Obviously this is not so in isolation.

The words below that relate to the different roots of rejection, can be used as a type of test or study to give an indication of a root of rejection. Go through every word quite quickly, taking an honest look at your character and personality to identify anything related to those words.

You can mark yourself on a scale of 0 to 5: 5 if this word really relates to you, to 0 if this word is really not you. It is important to discern how far you need to go back over the years. It is important to only go as far as the memory allows, and to avoid imagination and presumption.

As you add the marks in the word groupings, anything over 50% can be an indication of that specific root. It is important to involve someone close to you, in order to get his or her opinion and possible confirmation. It is vital to be honest.

Look at the three groupings of words which make up the fruit of rejection (there are obviously more). As you look at them and use them in your process of discerning roots, be sensitive and vulnerable to the Holy Spirit letting him pinpoint any weaknesses.

Remember too that some of these fruits may be demonic in their own right or they may be a reaction of the flesh, which will feed the roots of rejection. You must learn to discern and to trust the Holy Spirit, to direct you. If these areas are demonic, they can be dealt accordingly but remember discipleship will always be necessary.

Each word is given a definition to help understand the meaning.

FRUIT RELATING TO REBELLION OR REBELLIOUSNESS

Harshness:	Being severe, rough, usually verbally.
Rejection of others:	This can happen when rejected people come under pressure in relationships.
Hardness:	Strong, not easily penetrated, unyielding.
Unbelief:	Refusal or inability to believe, for, or in self.
Scepticism:	A strong or undermining attitude of doubt.
Defiance:	Hostile, resistant, openly disobedient.
Criticism:	Finding fault or imperfections.
Arrogance:	A feeling of superiority shown in an overbearing manner.
Stubbornness:	Will not give way, unyielding.
Anger:	Varied emotional reactions linked to loss of control.

Violence:	Either to self or others, words or actions.
Bitterness:	Full of resentment.
Drugs:	Any kind of medical substance or stimulant that may remove emotional pain.
Legalism:	An over emphasis of principle in any situation, i.e.
home or church.	
Occult	Any involvement is disobedience to God.
Lust:	Strong or excessive desire for power, recognition, ambition, materialism or sex.
Control:	Of yourself, emotions or domination of others.
Aggression:	Offensive, hostile.
Refusal of affection:	Will not accept comfort after felling rejected.
Argumentative:	Given to quarrels and disputes.
Revenge:	To retaliate, to pay back with word or deed.

FRUIT RELATING TO SELF REJECTION

Low self-image:	"I am of no value." Inferiority: "Everybody does it better than me."
Inadequacy:	"I can't."
Sadness:	An unhappy feeling, sometimes intense, mournful.
Sorrow:	Anguish or heartache due to loss.
Grief:	Deep or violent sorrow, great distress.
Shame:	A painful emotion related to one's own behaviour, disgrace or humiliation.
Guilt:	A feeling of doing something wrong.
Self-accusation:	"I am guilty, wrong." Putting self down.
Self-condemnation:	"I need to be punished." Cannot accept commendation.
Inability to communicate:	Something hindering communication, it may be stubbornness or sulking.

Fear of Failure:	"I can't cope with it happening again." Panic attack.
Insecurity:	Uncertain, unconfident.
Disappointment:	Failure to fulfil desires or expectations.
Loneliness:	"I have no one." Isolation.
Hopelessness:	"Its gone too far, there is no way out."
Wrong Expectations:	Assuming too much, or getting into wrong situations.
Seeking to please:	A pressure to please from a wrong motive.
Anxiety:	Troubled, uneasy, fretful.
Worry:	A continued or persistent torment.
Depression:	Dispirited, dejected, low heavy.
Infirmity:	Self-rejection can bring physical problems.

FRUIT RELATING TO SELF PROTECTION

Pressure to perform:	"I must be effective in order to gain acceptance."
Striving:	Trying too hard, conflict, strenuous effort.
Restlessness:	An internal drivenness, giving no rest.
Achieve:	"I must be successful in order to gain acceptance."
Competitiveness:	"I must be superior in all I do."
Independence:	"I can do without you, I can do it on my own"
Self-Centeredness:	"It's only me I'm interested in."
Self-Justification:	Always trying to make excuses for yourself.
Self Righteousness:	Always right, never wrong in own eyes.
Criticism of others:	Finding fault, disapproving, undermining.
Judgementalism:	A hurtful, hostile, injurious, authoritative pronouncement, often to or about someone
Jealousy:	Upset or angry with someone who is receiving what you want or need.
Envy:	A strong desire to have what someone else has.

Self-pity:	A feeling of sadness and sorrow for self.
Pride:	A high opinion of one's own qualities.
Possessiveness:	A strong desire to hold onto something or someone, linked to control.
Perfectionism:	"I must get it right." Faultless.
False Gratification:	Finding satisfaction or comfort, which only distracts from rejection, e.g. food, sex, nicotine, drink, drugs (illegal or prescribed).
Self-deception:	"I can't hear God", "no one understands me"
Fear of Betrayal:	'How can I trust anyone anymore.'
Unreality:	Withdrawal into a shell and avoidance of the problem
False Responsibility:	Taking on a responsibility that's not yours which leads to blame and false guilt.

Appendix 2

Some Questions Regarding Personal History

1. What is your first memory?
2. Were you wanted?
3. Was there an attempted abortion?
4. Did your birth follow a miscarriage or stillbirth?
5. Did your parents want a child of a different sex?
6. Was the birth traumatic?
7. Were you illegitimate?
8. What was your order of birth?
9. Are you an only child?
10. Were you and your mother able to bond?
11. Did she reject you?
12. Who brought you up?
13. How well did you know your father?
14. Was he away much?
15. Was there affection, touch and kiss from your father or mother or both?
16. What is your unhappiest family memory?
17. Who was the dominant force in your home?

18. What are the earliest memories you have of your parents?

19. How did your parents relate to each other?

20. Were there favourites in your family?

21. How were you disciplined?

22. Who disciplined you?

23. Did you feel your parents listened to you?

24. Were there favourites in your family?

25. Did you relate well to your siblings?

26. Did you try to get attention from your parents? How?

27. Was your father dominant, austere, severe or legalistic with you?

28. Did your parents put religious pressure on you?

29. Can you remember any negative words that were applied to you?

30. Are your parents separated or divorced? What happened to you?

31. Did you like school? Were there unhappy memories?

32. Did you go to a boarding school? At what age?

33. Do you like yourself?

34. Are you a regular eater?

35. Are there unusual eating habits in your family?

36. Have you ever thought about an overdose or suicide?

37. Do you have troubled sleep or nightmares? Are they consistent?

38. Do you have any unnatural or uncontrollable sexual thoughts or feelings?

39. Where did you learn about sex?

40. Have you engaged in pre or extra marital sexual activities?

41. Were you sexually abused?

42. Were you abused physically or mentally?

43. Have you any feelings of guilt

44. Do you feel unreasonably angry?

45. Do you struggle with feelings of shame?

46. Is there anyone you have difficulty in forgiving?

47. Have you experienced feelings of abandonment or isolation at having been let down or betrayed?

48. Do you relate well to authority figures?

49. Have you any habits you can't control?

50. Are you afraid of anything or anyone?

51. Have you felt dominated by your husband/wife or close relation?

52. Have you been in a failed marriage?

53. Do you feel the victim of the failure?

54. Do you feel discarded because of your failed marriage?

55. Have you been used or abused in your marriage?

56. Are you a single parent?

57. Do you feel hurt, misunderstood and rejected as one?

58. Do you feel discarded by the church?

59. Do you have a problem towards leadership in the church?

60. Do you find it difficult to make relationships in the church?

61. Have you felt you have let God and His church down?

62. Have you felt rejected by God because you have failed Him?

63. Have you been unemployed?

64. Have you been rejected for a job?

65. Do you long for affection and love?

66. Are you an emotional person?

67. Do you find it hard to express your emotions?

68. Do you think you cry too much?

69. Do you feel things deeply but can't express those feelings?

70. Do you love your family with actions or with words?

71. Do you know God's affirmation or do you feel the need to do more?

72. Do you say positive things to other people?

73. When in conversation, are you thinking about how to respond or do you listen?

74. Do you say what people want to hear in order to please them?

75. Do you have difficulty in taking people at face value?

76. Do you feel the need to justify yourself?

77. Do you find it difficult to apologise when you have done something wrong?

78. Do you think that if people knew your failings they would reject or abandon you?

79. Is God your "Abba" (Romans 8:15)?

My Orphan Heart

In writing this book I have made reference to the term "Orphan Heart", which I believe is an extensive subject in its own right. In view of this I am writing a companion book, which looks at the subject in more detail.

'My Orphan Heart' will include detailed testimony of how I came into a clear revelation of the Father's love. I talk about my early years when my parents hid so much from me, related to the circumstances of my birth. We look at, and understand, how that affected me over many years. This is mixed with some basic theology. Particular reference is made to our identity (who we are) and destiny (where we are going) as so much grows out of this.

The connection to rejection seems quite obvious and it is probable that, like me, many people have unknowingly lived with an orphan heart as well as rejection. Adam and Eve being banished from the Garden of Eden, left humanity exposed to the curse of rejection. It seems apparent that Adam orphaned himself as he made the choice to be with his bride, rather than stay with the Father as a son.

Jesus said, *"I will not leave you as orphans"* (John 14:18 NIV). This amazing statement makes clear the purpose of Jesus to bring reconciliation with the Father and restoration of sonship to the people of God. It also shows us how we can experience the Father's love and have a deep and intimate relationship with Him defined by the term "Abba".

'My Orphan Heart' is a testimony to the fact that by the grace of God an ordinary person can move from rejection to acceptance, from orphan to sonship and in doing so, come into a close relationship with God.